The Impossibility of Muslim Boyhood

(Continued on page 103)

The Impossibility of Muslim Boyhood

Shenila Khoja-Moolji

University of Minnesota Press

MINNEAPOLIS

LONDON

ISBN 978-1-5179-1719-7 (PB)
ISBN 978-1-4529-7102-5 (Ebook)
ISBN 978-1-4529-7240-4 (Manifold)

Published by the University of Minnesota Press, 2024
111 Third Avenue South, Suite 290
Minneapolis, MN 55401–2520
www.upress.umn.edu

Available as a Manifold edition at manifold.umn.edu

The University of Minnesota is an equal-opportunity educator and employer.

For my beloved MHI

Contents

1. Muslim Boyhood in America

IN JANUARY 2017, soon after Donald Trump's administration announced that visitors from seven predominantly Muslim countries would be denied entry into the United States, a five-year-old Muslim boy was handcuffed at Washington's Dulles airport. Airport security officers deemed the boy, whose name was not released, a "threat to America" and held him in custody for five hours.[1] Commenting on the incident, White House Press Secretary Sean Spicer said, "To assume that just because of someone's age and gender that they don't pose a threat would be misguided and wrong."[2] Just two years earlier, police had arrested fourteen-year-old Ahmed Mohamed at his school in Irving, Texas, for bringing a homemade digital clock to class. His English teacher thought it looked like a bomb. Law enforcement officers were called, and in a response that foreshadowed the later security overreach at the airport, Ahmed was handcuffed and taken to a juvenile detention center.

In both cases, the state response was disproportionate—disproportionate not only in its imaginative leap from actual to perceived threat, but also in the treatment these boys received when

---

1. Georgia Diebelius, "Boy, 5, Handcuffed at US Border for Being 'Security Threat' to USA," *Metro*, January 31, 2017, http://metro.co.uk/2017/01/31/boy-5-handcuffed-at-us-border-for-being-security-threat-to-usa-6417601/.
   2. Diebelius.

compared to what would have been meted out to similarly aged and similarly situated white boys. Ahmed's arrest at his school in Texas was the culmination of an organized school response, detailed in subsequent court filings:[3] the teacher confiscated the clock device, which was held in the school's administrative offices for several hours; the principal and a City of Irving police officer removed Ahmed from the classroom and escorted him to another room, where he was confronted by four or five more police officers and the school's counselor; the police questioned Ahmed for almost an hour and a half, and his pleas to call his parents were ignored. Even as Ahmed maintained that his device was a clock and not a bomb, the police officers handcuffed and arrested him; they transported him to the juvenile detention center where they took mugshots and fingerprints. This was an excessive response. Similarly, in the incident at Dulles airport, arresting a five-year-old boy, and then detaining him away from his mother, seems out of proportion, particularly when the only "triggering event" was the boy's racial and religious identity. Airport security articulated the boy as threatening in the absence of any action, or even the capacity for any action, that could rationally constitute a threat.

Examining instances of "mugging" by Black youth in Britain and the disproportionate public and state response to minor incidents of street harassment, Stuart Hall and his co-writers suggest in *Policing the Crisis* that "when such discrepancies appear between threat and reaction ... we have good evidence to suggest we are in the presence of an ideological displacement."[4] Writing in the context of moral panic, Hall thus mobilized the Freudian psychoanalytic notion of displacement, where a general unease about changing social roles

3. "Mohamed Elhassan Mohamed vs. Irving Independent School District Civil Action No. 3," United States District Court for the Northern District of Texas Dallas Division, May 18, 2017.

4. Stuart Hall, Chas Critcher, Tony Jefferson, John Clarke, and Brian Roberts, *Policing the Crisis: Mugging, the State, and Law and Order* (London: Palgrave Macmillan, 1978), 29.

or nebulous anxieties was being displaced onto Black youth. If we apply Hall's insight to present-day encounters between Muslim boys and the U.S. security apparatus, encounters like those I have described above, we might well ask: What ideological displacement are we witnessing? In the instances above, I would argue that it is the trauma of *past* terrorist attacks and anxiety surrounding imagined *future* attacks that is being displaced onto Muslim boys. The executive order that conjures the five-year-old boy as a "threat" asks that security officers at Dulles take multiple imaginative leaps: recall past terrorist attacks with Muslim perpetrators, visualize a future attack, and conceive of the little boy as a perpetrator in the present as well as in the future. However, since the five-year-old boy did not represent a tangible threat—and lacked capacity to do actual harm in an airport full of armed adults—we can understand these imaginative leaps, and the consequent invention of threat, as part of a broader ideological project that seeks to make future crime visible today, so it can be managed and eradicated through a sprawling carceral state. Anxieties about Muslim boys, then, relate only in the most limited of ways to actual Muslim boys and far more closely to the conceptual space of Muslim boyhood as a bridge between past terrorist events and events that might transpire in the future. In the process, though, Muslim boys are transformed into *proto*-terrorists or terrorists-in-the-making.

The construction of Muslim boys as proto-terrorists can be properly understood as a practice of racialization: it introduces impurity (threat) in the subject by disavowing the imputed purity (innocence) often associated with childhood. Here I draw on both Miriam Ticktin, who argues that political imaginations of innocence are shaped by a search for a "space of purity,"[5] and Deleuze and Guattari, who see race as another name for impurity conferred

5. Miriam Ticktin, "A World without Innocence," *America Ethnologist* 44, no. 4 (2017): 577.

by a system of domination.[6] While prior scholarly work on the racialization of Muslims has focused on adults, here we can extend that investigation by redirecting our attention to the experience of boyhood: the racialization of younger Muslims both draws on, and departs from, the racialization of adults. If boyhood is construed broadly as a developmental stage in the lifespan of a human, then Muslim boyhood is constructed as a developmental stage in the lifespan of a terrorist. And that perception is what distinguishes this category (and its racialization) from the racialization of Muslim adults generally in U.S. cultural framings.

Framing Muslim boys as proto-terrorists is politically useful in animating and sustaining a vigilant and vigilante stance toward a prospective war or terrorist attack. And since wars require preparation—weapons research and manufacturing, an ever-expanding militarily directed workforce, and surveillance—the threat implied in Muslim boyhood becomes an excuse for bloated expenditure on domestic and international security regimes. It justifies the expansion and privatization of security services, collaboration between military and police, investment in new technologies for surveillance, and the construction of new prisons and detention sites. A closer study of Muslim boyhood in public culture, then, not only reveals the routes and sites of racialization supplemental to those that are usually traced in scholarly inquiries, it also reminds us—as Cedric Robinson noted—that racialization is ultimately about the naturalization of capitalistic inequalities.[7] Accordingly, throughout the book, I suggest that the formulation of Muslim boyhood as a threat is tied to capitalist expansion and accumulation.

Carcerality in the United States, of course, has strong ties to anti-Blackness. As suggested by Michelle Alexander (among others),

6. Gilles Deleuze and Félix Guattari, *A Thousand Plateaus: Capitalism and Schizophrenia* (Minneapolis: University of Minnesota Press, 1987), 379.

7. Cedric Robinson, *Black Marxism* (Chapel Hill: University of North Carolina Press, 1983). On racial capitalism see Robin Kelley, "What Did Cedric Robinson Mean by Racial Capitalism?" *Boston Review,* January 12, 2017.

prisons are anti-Black institutions; they are designed that way.[8] But when we pay attention to Muslim boys, we come to understand how the War on Terror has inaugurated many changes to the U.S. carceral ecology, expanding the logics, sites, and forms of containment for a population defined on racial and national, as well as religious, terms. Agencies such as the Transportation Security Administration and programs like the FBI's Countering Violent Extremism were inaugurated after 9/11 to contain a threat explicitly defined as Muslim. We can see an expansion of the carceral ecology in detention rooms at airports and in temporary holding facilities at U.S. national borders; in the surveillance of Muslim Student Associations; in the recycling of combat equipment from military to local police forces (on full display in Ferguson, Miss., in August 2014 and in other U.S. cities since); in the Department of Homeland Security's Urban Areas Strategy Initiative and the Defense Department's 1122 Program, which allow police departments and sheriff's offices to purchase (through grant monies or their own funds) equipment at discounted federal prices. While not all of these changes have been exclusively targeted at Muslims, and Muslims are not the only individuals to be affected by them, the everyday surveillance of Muslims is an intended and significant outcome of this expansion. This surveillance can be understood as a portable form of enclosure: an additional dimension to the experience of carcerality in which the penitentiary has become mobile.

Relatedly, there is room to question whether the incidents above are provoked by race or religion. However, under my rubric of race (or racialization), such single-axis explanations of oppression are beside the point. The production of threat is not uniform; and different forms of threat (suicide bombing, hypersexuality, homicide, riots) are attached to different bodies, codifying them differently in the process. We therefore notice subtle variations in the expe-

8. Michelle Alexander, *The New Jim Crow* (New York: The New Press, 2012); see also Simone Browne, *Dark Matters: On the Surveillance of Blackness* (Durham, N.C.: Duke University Press, 2015).

riences of Black as compared to Brown or white or white-passing Muslim boys; immigrants as compared to American-born Muslims; working-class Muslims as compared to those who are captains of industry. As we will see in the case of the "Boston Marathon bomber" in chapter 3, white-passing can mitigate anti-Muslim sentiment; Brownness might amplify it. It is, therefore, more helpful to think of these regimes of difference (religion, race, caste, class, or ethnicity) as connective, with those connections in turn adding to their intensity and force. Thus, when I narrate episodes of violence, I resist the temptation to outline which specific regime of difference is in play. Race, Islam, and ethnicity are more helpfully viewed as assemblages, and I consider how various regimes of difference solidify, mix, and overlap, in specific spatiotemporal contexts, to demarcate otherness.[9] It is by focusing on connected histories and associations within apparently distinct regimes of difference that we are able to better understand how racialization proceeds.

And Muslims have always been part of this story of race in America. If, as Renisa Mawani argues, race is a "modern regime that instituted an entire range of differences (historical, corporeal, cultural, climatic, and moral) between Europeans [and] non-Europeans,"[10] then Shaista Patel has also shown that European encounters with African and Arab Muslims (pejoratively called Moors) on the Iberian Peninsula were constitutive in this project of instituting difference. The eight centuries of Muslim and African presence in Europe became the lens through which Europeans, beginning in the fifteenth century, viewed the people they invaded in the "New World."[11] Since Europe had long defined its identity and its

9. On racializing assemblages see Alexander Weheliye, *Habeas Viscus* (Durham, N.C.: Duke University Press, 2014).

10. Renisa Mawani, "Specters of Indigeneity in British-Indian Migration, 1914," *Law & Society Review* 46, no. 2 (2012): 373.

11. Shaista Patel, "The 'Indian Queen' of the Four Continents: Tracing the 'Undifferentiated Indian' through Europe's Encounters with Muslims, Anti-Blackness, and Conquest of the 'New World,'" *Cultural Studies* 33, no. 3 (2019): 417.

purity against a Moorish foil, European views of indigenous people, and later of enslaved people and migrants, would be informed by prevailing discourses of Muslim otherness. In fact, as David Theo Goldberg has observed, "Race of necessity is knotted from the outset of its formulation and social fashioning with religious resonance. Jews, Muslims, and black and New World Indian 'heathens' represent Europe's formative nonbelonging."[12] Distancing between the dominant group and others ultimately pushes the non-belonging person or group into the experience of racism.

I do not, however, intend in this book to offer an essentialized description of Muslim boyhood—indeed, there is no single essential experience. Instead, I view Muslim boyhood as a heuristic device,[13] one that highlights for us how constructions of threat are integral to the story of American racial capitalism. The figure of the proto-terrorist—created and reproduced through ordinary practices of surveillance at schools and at airports, as I show in chapter 2—is a capitalist necessity, used to harness public alertness in relation to a prefigured future-attack and to keep America in a permanent state of war. But racial capitalism takes other routes as well. In chapter 3, I discuss the instrumental staging of Muslim boys by state and media elites, which allows them a tentative entry into the domain of innocence so others can profit from them. When Ahmed Mohamed is invited to the White House or on a tour of the New York City Hall, politicians see an opportunity to represent themselves as antiracists and buy public goodwill, in a practice I term *commodity antiracism*. Such ostensibly positive portrayals of Muslim boys work through

12. David Theo Goldberg, "Militarizing Race," *Social Text* 34, no. 4 (2016): 19.

13. I follow the lead of Alys Weinbaum et al. as they use the heuristic device of the 'modern girl' to investigate geographically and politically specific manifestations of the modern girl while nonetheless observing connections and similarities that extend across different iterations. See Alys Weinbaum, Lynn Thomas, Priti Ramamurthy, Uta Poiger, Madeleine Yue Dong, and Tani Barlow, *The Modern Girl around the World* (Durham, N.C.: Duke University Press, 2008).

exception and preserve the collective notion of Muslim boyhood as a condition of threat and impurity.

As the brief digression above into European history reminds us, an American construction of Muslim boyhood partakes in a long history and exists in parallel to iterations of Muslim boyhood as they have developed in other global settings. If Muslim boyhood is, in the U.S., a heuristic device against which the center—defined as pure, innocent, or non-raced—becomes manifest, then we might ask what this device reveals in other societies where Muslims are minoritized or politically and socially marginalized. I conclude by briefly considering India as that other context: a site where we see emerge a similar focus on Islam and boyhood as threatening or contaminating elements. The place that whiteness fills as a salient racializing force in the U.S. is, in the case of India, occupied by the Hindutva ideology. We can see parallels between the American construction of the proto-terrorist and Hindu fears of the "love jihadi." While the specific manifestations of Muslim boyhood may vary in different global settings, it is worth noting the recurring negative cultural attention directed toward Muslim boys, in particular, and the determination to distance them from the state of innocence that more often attaches to childhood. By conceptualizing Muslim boyhood as a heuristic, we can begin to see linkages across political contexts, even as Muslim boyhood is networked with different locally specific ideologies.

Race and Religion as a Connective Regime

Racism in America, as Michael Omi and Howard Winant have explained, has a strong visual dimension, which entails ascribing "social and symbolic meaning to perceived phenotypical differences."[14] In recent times, racism has extended to incorporate cultural traits.

14. Michael Omi and Howard Winant, *Racial Formation in the United States* (New York: Routledge, 1994), 111.

Amaney Jamal argues that today's racialization of Arabs and Muslims perceives a "clash of values . . . This process of 'othering' is based on assumptions about culture and religion instead of phenotype."[15] In these newly cultural practices of racialization, Saher Selod observes that the usual markers of racial difference, such as skin color, have been replaced by cultural markers—the hijab, a beard, or a Muslim-sounding name.[16] When the practice of othering is expanded from phenotypes to encompass culture, Islam (a religion that, like other religions, is lived in part through sartorial choices and visible, everyday behaviors) is racialized as a result.[17] And racialization here has spatial dimensions, defining Islam in terms of its perceived *distance* from white liberal humanism. Deleuze and Guattari explain:

> Racism operates by the determination of degrees of deviance in relation to the White-Man face, which endeavors to integrate nonconforming traits into increasingly eccentric and backward waves, sometimes tolerating them at given places under given conditions, in a given ghetto, sometimes erasing them from the wall, which never abides alterity (it's a Jew, it's an Arab, it's a Negro, it's a lunatic . . .). From the viewpoint of racism, there is no exterior, there are no people on the outside. There are only people who should be like us and whose crime it is not to be.[18]

15. Amaney Jamal, "Civil Liberties and the Otherization of Arab and Muslim Americans," in *Race and Arab Americans before and after 9/11*, ed. Amaney Jamal and Nadine Naber (Syracuse, N.Y.: Syracuse University Press, 2008), 119.

16. Saher Selod, "Citizenship Denied: The Racialization of Muslim American Men and Women Post-9/11," *Critical Sociology* 41, no. 1 (2015): 77–95.

17. See Saher Selod and David Embrick, "Racialization and Muslims: Situating the Muslim Experience in Race Scholarship," *Sociology Compass* 7, no. 8 (2013): 644–55; Tariq Modood, *Multicultural Politics: Racism, Ethnicity, and Muslims in Britain* (Minneapolis: University of Minnesota Press, 2005); Andrew Shyrock, "The Moral Analogies of Race," in *Race and Arab Americans Before and After 9/11*, ed. Amaney Jamal and Nadine Naber (Syracuse, N.Y.: Syracuse University Press, 2008), 81–113.

18. Deleuze and Guattari, *A Thousand Plateaus,* 178.

In "should be like us" and the crime of "not to be," we see a center defined in terms of purity, with deviation expressed as distance from that pure center. To the extent that Islam is distanced from whiteness (Deleuze and Guattari's "White-Man face"), its practitioners are moved from "non-raced" to "raced." The categories of "Islam" and "race" are thus conceptually linked to each other in a place progressively marked by impurity ("eccentric and backward waves"). As Deleuze and Guattari argue, "The race-tribe exists only at the level of an oppressed race, and in the name of the oppression it suffers: there is no race but inferior, minoritarian; there is no dominant race; a race is defined not by its purity but rather by the impurity conferred upon it by a system of domination."[19] In the context of Muslim boyhood, then, this leads us to ask the question that naturally emerges from this definition of race: How is this impurity conferred and maintained? Considering rhetorical strategies around purity/impurity—which, as we have seen above, are often discussed through notions of innocence and threat—may reveal the way this distribution is effected and policed.

We see these dynamics in the casting of Muslim men as "a mutilated deviation from proper [read White] manhood," as Gargi Bhattacharyya has suggested.[20] Mariam Durrani's close reading of the conservative American website *Breitbart News* shows that Muslim men appear on the website primarily as sexual predators and as un/sub-human, often labeled as Neanderthals, pigs, or vermin.[21] In *Breitbart*'s heavily fictionalized narrative, Durrani sees Muslim men portrayed as engaging in violence not only against non-Muslims (associations with terrorist attacks) but also against their own daughters (accusations of rape). *Breitbart*'s discourse is

19. Deleuze and Guattari, 379.

20. Gargi Bhattacharyya, *Dangerous Brown Men* (New York: Zed Books, 2008), 89.

21. Mariam Durrani, "The Gendered Muslim Subject," in *The Oxford Handbook of Language and Race,* ed. H. Samy Alim (Oxford: Oxford University Press, 2020), 353.

an extreme expression of assumptions that exist more broadly in U.S. society, where Muslim men are often presented as fully formed terrorists and predators. But when a five-year-old Iranian-American Muslim boy is arrested at an airport, it is not about any actual acts of violence; it is the *potentiality* that he represents. Scrutiny of this potentially violent group might even exceed that of the scrutiny directed at adults. In a focus group formed for this project (which will feature in chapter 2), a teenaged boy put it this way: "This age range that we are in, like I am guessing he [Ahmed Mohamed] is around our age too? People assume that we are more reckless since we are not completely mature yet, until we reach a certain age. So, they think we would be more capable of doing these things than, say, a forty-year-old." Capability and potentiality orient us toward the future. In the imaginary of the security regime (of which the security officers at Dulles are an instantiation), Muslim boys are presumed perpetrators of future terrorist attacks: they are imagined as proto-terrorists. And since they might turn violent at any moment, logic dictates that they must be quarantined or at least regarded with suspicion. The detection and enclosure of the proto-terrorist will be the topic of the next chapter.

But not all Muslims are imputed with impurity (or distanced from the center) similarly. If we follow Deleuze and Guattari in recognizing that racism establishes degrees of deviance, with some bodies coded as more distant from the center than others, then we must recognize that Black, Brown, white, and white-passing Muslims experience the process of racialization differently. In addition, this experience of racialization can change as the context or conditions change. In some instances, Muslimness can overwhelm whiteness: Patrick Casey studied white converts to Islam who experienced prejudice only when they donned Muslim religious markers, such as hijab for women or kufi for men.[22] Similarly, given the close visual

---

22. Patrick Casey, "The Racialization of American Muslim Converts by the Presence of Religious Markers," *Ethnicities* 21, no. 3 (2021): 521–37.

association of race and religion, and the use of cultural markers in the process of racialization, those who "look like" Muslims, such as Sikhs, may also be subject to hate crimes. The first anti-Muslim hate crime in the aftermath of 9/11 was committed against a Sikh man in Arizona. The victim was working at his gas station when a forty-two-year-old white man drove up and shot him five times before fleeing the scene. When we consider race and Islam as belonging to a connective regime (and include other axes of difference such as gender, age, or nationality), we can observe the uneven assignment of impurity/threat that is subject to change under given conditions. We can thus account for variation in individual experiences of racialization without relinquishing the notion that there exists a shared minoritarian sense. Here, I am informed by José Muñoz's use of "feeling" and "sense," where the former is linked to an individual experience and the latter in relation to experiencing that feeling as part of a commons.[23]

The Promise and Perils of Innocence

In a broader U.S. cultural context, where childhood is typically equated with innocence, how do we understand incidents like the ones discussed at the beginning of this chapter? How is it that five- and fourteen-year-old Muslim boys are arrested for actions that would normally be overlooked or even praised, or detained for simply existing?

Modern societies insist on certain ideas about childhood. Prominent among these is the link between childhood and innocence. The *Oxford English Dictionary* accordingly defines children as "free from moral wrong, sin, or guilt"; to be a child is to be "pure, unpolluted." But until recently childhood was not associated with purity. Robin Bernstein notes that in the U.S. historical context, the

23. José Esteban Muñoz, *The Sense of Brown* (Durham, N.C.: Duke University Press, 2000).

doctrine of childhood innocence emerged only in the late eighteenth and nineteenth centuries.[24] Children, including white children, were previously seen as inherently sinful and sexual—born with original sin and thus not innocent—as well as lacking the rationality and self-control that would come to them as adults. Nineteenth-century thinkers reimagined children as innocent—without sin, without sexual feelings, oblivious to worldly affairs, and potentially able to redeem adults. Children were, Bernstein argues, "understood not as innocent but as innocence itself; not as a symbol of innocence but as its embodiment."[25] In the contemporary American context, images of childhood innocence are often deployed to invoke pure, unpolluted spacetimes—nostalgia about a pristine past or longing for a peaceful future. Ticktin accordingly notes that political imaginations of innocence are shaped by a search for a "space of purity."[26]

To ensure that childhood remains a politically useful space for recalling the past and imagining the future, "child fundamentalism" holds that children must remain unsullied by politics, sin, corruption, and sexual knowledge.[27] In other words, children must remain pure and protecting childhood innocence by ensuring that they are not exposed to certain knowledge and experiences thus becomes a societal imperative. Ticktin locates this formulation of innocence in the Judeo-Christian tradition of Adam and Eve, a story where innocence is linked to lack of worldly knowledge; Adam and Eve's fall from the garden of Eden follows from Eve's decision to eat from the tree of knowledge.[28] Innocence is thus defined by deficit and lack: of knowledge, agency, and experience. But this deficit-state

24. Robin Bernstein, *Racial Innocence* (New York: New York University Press, 2011).

25. Bernstein, 4.

26. Ticktin, "A World without Innocence," 577.

27. The term "child fundamentalism" is used by Barbara Baird to describe this insistence on protecting children from corruption. Barbara Baird, "Child Politics, Feminist Analyses," *Australian Feminist Studies* 23, no. 57 (2008): 291–305.

28. Ticktin, "A World without Innocence," 579.

does not lead to entry into the "space of purity" for everyone as differently racialized populations are situated differently in relation to this space.

The reimagined nineteenth-century childhood was racially coded as white and was constituted in opposition to Blackness: the Black child was marked as non-innocent and as a laboring body subject to discipline. Significantly, even where innocence was imputed to Black people, it did not automatically lead to freedom, or to forgiveness, as it would for white children. Defenders of chattel slavery, as Erica Meiners has observed, equated Black adults with children narrowly in terms of their ability to reason, and did so to legitimize disciplining enslaved adults.[29] Abolitionists, for their part, invoked adult Blacks' supposed childlike status to argue for their better treatment: if not capable of adult reason, they should be punished less harshly.[30] Innocence (mobilized as a deficit state) thus has had paradoxical consequences for Black people: it has been used to advance both violent regulation and care, to justify discipline and control of child and adult populations. More recently, presumed childish irrationality has been deployed both to advance the carceral state (building prisons to discipline unreason) and to advocate for abolishing the prison system (rehabilitation instead of punishment).[31]

In the twenty-first-century Western context, nonwhite boys are typically assumed to be more precocious and sexually experienced, an assumption that prevents their association with innocence and, relatedly, prevents their entry into the space of purity. This Western tendency to project greater maturity onto nonwhite boys was apparent during the recent refugee crisis in Europe. In 2015, when the body of a three-year-old Syrian boy—Aylan Kurdi, who drowned in the Mediterranean Sea—washed up on a beach in Turkey, it sparked

29. Erica Meiners, *For the Children? Protecting Innocence in a Carceral State* (Minneapolis: University of Minnesota Press, 2016).

30. Bernstein, *Racial Innocence*, 25.

31. Meiners, *For the Children?*, 5.

widespread public concern for refugees in Europe. Public sentiment in the United Kingdom and the European Union strengthened
in support of welcoming more refugees, especially children. The
following year, after a campaign led by Labour politician Alfred
Dubs, new legislation was introduced in Britain to permit entry
for unaccompanied refugee children. While the proposal asked
for the admission of 3,000 children, permission was given only
for 350 (a number later increased to 480). Nevertheless, as Carly
McLaughlin notes, when nonwhite youth actually arrived under the
proposed law's provisions for children and youth up to age eighteen, the welcoming sentiments quickly transformed into scrutiny
and suspicion.[32] These young boys arriving from the Middle East
departed from the model of the lonely child; they were burly and
tall; some had facial hair and wore hoodies. They were therefore
read as "unchildlike children" and "foreign delinquents."[33] It was
insinuated that adults had forged their documents to gain entry as
youth. Because they did not fit an unstated model of visible childlike innocence, some incoming youth—many Muslim boys among
them—were not deemed worthy of protection.

Just a few years later, for Ukrainian refugees—coded as white
(albeit precariously)—fleeing to the United Kingdom following
Russia's February 2022 invasion, childlike innocence expanded to
incorporate adults as well. Media coverage of Ukrainian refugees
often featured girls and women, emphasizing notions of vulnera-
bility and lack of facility in the English language, which made them
worthy of care. A feature article on *BBC News,* for example, portrays
white women and girls photographed against natural terrains of
tranquil streams, grassy meadows, and fluffy sheep.[34] Media com-

32. Carly McLaughlin, "They Don't Look Like Children': Child
Asylum-Seekers, the Dubs Amendment, and the Politics of Childhood,"
Journal of Ethnic and Migration Studies 44, no. 11 (2018): 1757–73.

33. McLaughlin, 1 and 7.

34. Martin Dan Martin and Jennifer Harby, "How Ukrainian Refugees
Found Their Second Home in the UK," *BBC News,* February 23, 2023,
https://www.bbc.com/news/uk-england-derbyshire-64676216.

mentators explicitly compared Ukrainian refugees with those from the Middle East: a senior foreign correspondent at *CBS News* said, Kyiv "isn't a place, with all due respect, like Iraq or Afghanistan, that has seen conflict raging for decades. This is a relatively civilized, relatively European—I have to choose those words carefully, too—city, one where you wouldn't expect that, or hope that it's going to happen."[35] A former British politician writing for the *Telegraph* remarked: "They seem so like us. That is what makes it so shocking. Ukraine is a European country. Its people watch Netflix and have Instagram accounts, vote in free elections, and read uncensored newspapers."[36] And, on *BBC News,* a former deputy prosecutor of Ukraine said: "It's very emotional for me because I see European people with blue eyes and blonde hair being killed."[37]

For Ukrainian refugees, the U.K. Home Office simplified visa forms, fully digitized the visa process, removed certain routine eligibility criteria related to language requirements and salary thresholds, and boosted staff numbers so applications could be processed quickly. Sponsorship schemes such as "Homes for Ukraine" and the "Ukraine Family Scheme" were created to encourage individuals and businesses to take in, host, house, and provide homes for refugees. According to Department of Levelling Up, Housing and Communities, Ukrainian refugees had "the right to work and to access benefits and public services, including education and health-

35. Charlie D'Agata cited in Ben Kesslen, "CBS News' Charlie D'Agata Apologizes for Saying Ukraine More 'Civilized' than Iraq, Afghanistan," *New York Post,* February 26, 2022, https://nypost.com/2022/02/26/cbs -news-charlie-dagata-apologizes-for-saying-ukraine-more-civilized-than -iraq-afghanistan/.

36. Daniel Hannan, "Vladimir Putin's Monstrous Invasion Is an Attack on Civilisation Itself," *Telegraph,* February 26, 2022, https://www.telegraph .co.uk/news/2022/02/26/vladimir-putins-monstrous-invasion-attack -civilisation/.

37. Arab News, "Interview," *YouTube,* March 1, 2022, https://www .youtube.com/watch?v=pU-8gKaUO_Y.

care, on the same footing as U.K. nationals."[38] By the end of June 2023, more than 179,500 people from Ukraine had arrived in the United Kingdom.[39] Such is the reception of whiteness: it is welcomed, accommodated, facilitated, and supported. This is not, of course, to deny that Ukrainians are precariously situated within whiteness. Daria Krivonos has observed that before the full-scale Russian onslaught, Ukrainians who migrated to Poland for work did not experience the same protections as their European counterparts; they were "denied access to complete or 'hegemonic' whiteness."[40] And yet, without negating the variegated experience of people coded as white, we can notice shared white privilege; we can further see how racialized Muslims (and Muslim nations) serve as a foil for Ukrainian innocence, whiteness, and civilization. Krivonos herself notes that preference and favorable treatment of Ukrainians should be situated in a context of widespread anti-Muslim and anti-Black racism.

In the United States, the politics of innocence often plays out in a judicial or carceral context; we may see reduced cultural attention to childlike purity or innocence in the abstract but a heightened awareness of how ascribed maturity (or lack thereof) relates to innocence of—or responsibility for—one's actions. White children and adults alike are afforded a lack of culpability that is usually associated with innocence. Analyzing reports from the trial of U.S. army personnel who engaged in sexual violence at Abu Ghraib,

38. Department of Levelling Up, Housing and Communities, "100,000 Ukrainians Welcomed to Safety in the UK," *Government of United Kingdom,* July 28, 2022, https://www.gov.uk/government/news/100000-ukrainians -welcomed-to-safety-in-the-uk.

39. United Kingdom Home Office, "Statistics on Ukrainians, Year Ending June 2023," *Government of United Kingdom,* https://www.gov.uk /government/statistics/immigration-system-statistics-year-ending-june -2023/statistics-on-ukrainians-in-the-uk.

40. Daria Krivonos, "Racial Capitalism and the Production of Difference in Helsinki and Warsaw," *Journal of Ethnic and Migration Studies* 49, no. 6 (2023): 1509.

Kelly Oliver wonders why soldiers who perpetrated acts of torture were dismissed as teenagers "just having fun."[41] She suggests their horrible acts were normalized as childish fun because imputing childhood innocence to the perpetrators served as an "inoculant against responsibility and guilt."[42] This inoculant effect was especially visible when Abu Ghraib defendants claimed not to know that forcing Muslim prisoners to eat pork violated their religious beliefs: they tried to enter the domain of innocence by way of ignorance.

While Oliver writes specifically about torture at Abu Ghraib, white innocence is similarly imputed in many of the incidents involving Muslim boys that I describe in this book. A particularly disturbing example of this innocence-ignorance nexus comes to us from Lynnwood, Washington. On November 6, 2021, a thirteen-year-old Muslim boy was brutally beaten and dragged from place to place on the streets of Lynnwood by two teens (fifteen and thirteen years old), who also hurled insults about his mother, calling her a "Muslim terrorist."[43] During the hour-long assault, one of the attackers asked the boy to "kiss his shoes and perform the act of prostration [as done during the Muslim prayer]." The act of prostration in an Islamic religious context is an expression of ultimate submission to the Divine. In asking the boy to perform prostration, the perpetrators both mocked Islam and demanded submission: a demand that lays claim to power and simultaneously establishes a symbolic boundary between the one who submits and the one submitted to. The intentionality of this act seems evident, but was it obvious to the society that was responsible for punishing these offenders? We often see that these intentions are obscured in the aftermath of such acts. In claiming innocence (or engaging in willful

41. Kelly Oliver, "Innocence, Perversion, and Abu Ghraib," *Philosophy Today* 51, no. 3 (2007): 346.

42. Oliver, 347.

43. Jake Goldstein-Street, "Teens Charged with Hate Crime in Islamophobic Attack near Lynnwood," *Herald Net,* March 25, 2022, https://www.heraldnet.com/news/teens-charged-with-hate-crime-in -islamophobic-attack-near-lynnwood/.

ignorance), the perpetrators of torture or bullying, or those who quarantined the five-year-old boy at the airport, shield themselves from accountability. When army guards "don't know" that pork is offensive to Muslim sensibilities; when the teacher "doesn't realize" the device is a homemade clock; when the teens who force the Muslim boy to prostrate are "just playing around," we can see the innocence-ignorance nexus at work.

But there is also a second, more broadly culturally damning reality: that the white soldiers or bullying teens might not in fact fully understand the meaning of their bullying (though of course they understand it in part), because the U.S. educational system does not pay much attention to teaching about Islam.[44] Perpetrators can claim innocence because as a society we do not ensure that ignorance is not an option, that students grow up in a diverse culture knowing basic information about their neighbors.

In tracing the politics of innocence, I do not intend to claim (or reclaim) innocence for Muslim boys. The quest for innocence inevitably leads to redemptive or respectability politics and not to transformative justice. This book is not a defense of innocence. I am instead interested in understanding how societies distribute innocence, how they map it onto certain bodies and withhold it from others, and the consequences of those projects of distribution and ascription. When innocence is denied to Muslim boys, they are refused permission to experiment or to make mistakes. Experimentation's relationship to boyhood as a developmental stage is complex: boyhood evokes an expectation of experimentation and frivolity, but also the anticipation of discipline from adults. The particular construction of Muslim boyhood as a threat means that Muslim boys may well experience the disciplinary aspect of boyhood, but they certainly do not have permission to experiment or to be wrong. This bifurcation of expected boyhood experienc-

44. On the teaching of Islam in American schools see Natasha Merchant, "Teaching about Islam in U.S. Schools," *Thresholds* 41, no. 2 (2018): 64–67.

es is vividly illustrated in the punitive school and state response when Ahmed brought his clock to school. Muslim boys are a priori assumed to be terrorists, carrying the *potential* for terror—and this imputed future disqualifies them from partaking in the pleasures and freedoms of boyhood. This denial has further material consequences for them in the form of everyday bullying and surveillance. Muslim boys then grow up learning to make themselves small and invisible to evade the white disciplinary gaze.

Archives of Muslim Boyhood

While much has been written about the racialization of Muslims in America, scholars have only recently begun to pay greater attention to its gendered dimensions.[45] Incorporating gender into our analysis helps us to see not only how women, men, and non-binary people are racialized differently but also how anti-Muslim practices interact with other regimes of difference, including sexuality, ability, national origin, and social class. The emerging work on gender and racialization has, however, focused on adult Muslims, particularly women. There is good reason for this: the trope of the "oppressed Muslim woman" has often been mobilized as an excuse for colonial and imperial invasions of Muslim-majority regions. Studies about Muslim youth, on the other hand, have tended to center on their lived experiences as religious minorities in the West, including struggles with belonging and identity, and experiences of bullying.[46]

45. See as an example Durrani, "The Gendered Subject." A number of Muslim scholars and activists, most notably Jasmine Zine and Darakshan Raja, have begun to theorize the gendered effects of anti-Muslim violence.

46. Empirical studies include: Louise Archer, "Race, 'Face,' and Masculinity," in *Muslims in Britain,* ed. Peter Hopkins and Richard Gale (Edinburgh: Edinburgh University Press, 2009), 74–91; Louise Archer, *Race, Masculinity, and Schooling* (London: McGraw Hill, 2003); Farzana Shain, *The New Folk Devils* (Stoke-on-Trent, UK: Trentham Books, 2011); Luke Howie, Amanda Keddie, Lucas Walsh, and Jane Wilkinson, "Wild and Tame Zones in Times of Disharmony," *Australia, Journal of Youth Studies* 24, no. 7

While questions of experience and political figuration are inter-linked, this book focuses on the latter as it can help us recognize the gamut of subjective experiences available for those who identify as Muslim boys. And, as it turns out, the available subject positions are not particularly hospitable.

Considering Muslim boyhood in the United States means ex-amining the discursive practices through which the figure of the Muslim boy appears in our world: the speech acts, institutional policies, behaviors, and norms that bring this subject into effect and the historical conditions that make it possible. Specifically, I study how Muslim boyhood takes shape in particular spaces (in schools, at borders, and in mass media) and within specific relations (encoun-ters with the police or FBI, interactions with teachers and white peers). No single location or relation is determining, but we can detect a pattern across these sites and networks as U.S. public cul-ture is formed and expressed. Episodes of arrests, bullying, killing, and surveillance of Muslim boys are my objects of analysis. Events investigated include the following: the 2015 arrest of fourteen-year-old Ahmed Mohamed at his school in Irving, Texas; the 2016 beating of a sixteen-year-old on the streets outside a Muslim community center in Brooklyn; the 2016 alleged abuse and assault of an eleven-year-old (publicly identified only as A.A.) by his teacher Faye Myles in Phoenix; the 2016 beating of seven-year-old Abdul Aziz on a school bus in North Carolina; the 2017 arrest of a five-year-old at Washington's Dulles airport; the 2021 beating of a thirteen-year-old Muslim boy on the streets of Lynnwood, Washington; and the 2022 death of fourteen-year-old Afghan refugee Rezwan Kohistani in Missouri. Throughout the book I identify the boys by their first

(2021): 871–85; Studies on Muslim girls include Farzana Shain, "Navigating the Unequal Education Space in Post-9/11 England," *Educational Philosophy and Theory* 53, no. 3 (2021): 270–87; Tehmina Basit, "I Want More Freedom, but Not Too Much: British Muslim Girls and the Dynamism of Family Values," *Gender and Education* 9, no. 4 (1997): 425–40; Heidi Mirza and Veena Meetoo, "Empowering Muslim Girls?" *British Journal of Sociology of Education* 39, no. 2 (2018): 227–41.

name; this is partly to humanize them and also a way of recognizing how very young they are. I extend my analysis via a close study of FBI policies developed with the specific goal of intervening in school settings where extremist recruitment is anticipated—the FBI's Preventing Violent Extremism in Schools program. In this program's educator-facing materials, we can see the precise mechanisms that turn a cautionary discourse on extremism toward the construction of Muslim boyhood as a threat.

While I will have a lot to say about violence against Muslim boys, I will disrupt that by talking about those rare moments when they are staged as innocent or given celebrity status. These are episodes that escape the ubiquitous enfolding of Muslim boys into stereotypes associated with Muslim men. In one such instance, Ahmed Mohamed is first arrested for his homemade alarm clock, but then is invited to visit the White House and Facebook headquarters. Such staging, which seems contradictory and at least initially a deviation from the pattern we see so often, I argue, ultimately fails to challenge the original frames. It works through exception, which entails abstracting Muslim boys (segregating and elevating the one from all), whereas the negative portrayals of Muslims that we will encounter work through aggregation (subsuming the one within all). Instrumental staging of Muslim boys like Ahmed enables politicians and corporations to buy goodwill by articulating themselves as antiracists, in a practice I name: commodity antiracism. In another case, a white-passing Muslim youth, Dzhokhar Tsarnaev, kills three people and injures hundreds at the 2013 Boston Marathon and ends up featured on the cover of *Rolling Stone* magazine. Here we see another example of instrumental staging where a corporation breaks away from sedimented frames of Muslim boyhood in the service of profit/revenue. In these cases, we see how terrorism is commercialized and antiracism commodified.

Although this book is a cultural critique and I remain focused on public culture, my thinking is also informed by five focus group interviews with twenty-six non-white Muslim high school boys, conducted in the aftermath of the 2017 Dulles airport arrest. The interviews took place in Queens, New York, between April and June of 2017, during an afterschool program for high school boys run by a local nonprofit youth development organization. I co-conducted the interviews with a staff member (a Muslim man of Pakistani heritage) who had been working with the participants since 2015. Participants were mostly recent immigrants from Bangladesh, Nepal, and Pakistan, or second-generation Americans whose parents had migrated from these countries. They were mostly Brown and Muslim; on one occasion a couple of non-Muslim boys of color participated in the discussions as well.[47] Study participants did not want to be identified by their names, so I use pseudonyms for them. The arrest of the five-year-old boy at Dulles airport earlier that year and Ahmed Mohamed's arrest just two years prior were the primary topics of our discussion. I wanted to see how these boys reacted to the cases: Could these same overreactions have happened to them? Could the same have happened to a girl? These conversations led us to more intimate exchanges about how my interlocutors navigated everyday life: participants compared the relative safety of their predominantly Brown schools and neighborhoods with experiences they had in Manhattan or other "white neighborhoods," where "as the only Brown person, the cop is just looking at you." Findings from these focus groups contextualize the isolated encounters featured elsewhere in the book. They show us how Muslim boys encounter and negotiate the political formation of Muslim boyhood at the heart of this book through minor gestures ("avoiding eye contact," "taking a different street," "staying mellow," "not draw[ing] attention to yourself"). We can see in these moments how oppressive constructions are

47. I was directed to this afterschool program because a cohort of Brown Muslim boys regularly attended it. However, since the program was open to all high school boys at the school, on one occasion a couple of non-Muslim boys of color attended as well. Out of respect, I did not ask them to leave.

experienced in everyday life as burdens and burdening, crushing the bodies of Muslim boys into an ever-smaller space.

Following Frantz Fanon, Sylvia Wynter, and Simone Brown, I direct attention toward the circulation of Muslim boyhood in public culture (where it becomes a signifier for threat), the fact of Muslim boyhood (where young Muslim life is an objective fact), and the varied experience of Muslim boyhood (where different regimes of impurity intersect to shape this experience).[48] Even as I try to parse these out in the chapters below for analytical clarity, their entanglement is patently clear. I close with a reflection on what the heuristic of Muslim boyhood reveals when analyzed in a different global context, that of India under the current Hindu supremacist ideology. We see at work similar anxieties about purity and assumptions of innocence/threat, not in relation to whiteness but in relation to ethno-religious absolutism. These anxieties are nonetheless given shape and force through a discourse about, and surveillance of, Muslim boys.

This book began as an investigation about the politics of innocence in relation to Muslim boys, but I end up telling a much broader story of how Muslim boyhood in the American context ties together white supremacy, carceral ecologies, and capitalist accumulation. I tell this story out of a concern for the people who can get caught in this violent matrix. And by viewing Muslim boyhood as a heuristic, we can analyze its manifestation in other contexts as well, revealing both continuities and differences. Reading about violence against Muslims boys in the media and court documents, or in communications from my interlocutors; watching videos of beatings and harassment; following hashtag campaigns where indi-

48. Frantz Fanon, *Black Skin, White Masks*, trans. Charles Markmann (London: Pluto Press, 1986); Sylvia Wynter, "Towards the Sociogenic Principle: Fanon, Identity, the Puzzle of Conscious Experience, and What It Is Like to Be 'Black,'" in *National Identities and Sociopolitical Changes in Latin America*, ed. Mercedes F. Dúran-Cogan and Antonio Gómez-Moriana (New York: Routledge, 2001), 30–66; Browne, *Dark Matters*.

viduals reveal their experiences of abuse and intimidation; paying attention to the perpetrators' side: these are all difficult experiences. But attention to the specifics—words, feelings, photographs, and so on—is important because, as Ghassem-Fachandi observes, it is precisely through the practices of naming, labeling, staging, and describing that some spaces, bodies, and objects are purified, and others are cast as impure.[49] And that which gets cast as impure— through assertions of threat, underdevelopment, criminality, excess emotion, or backwardness—as history has shown, gets colonized, expropriated, and even eradicated.

---

49. Parvis Ghassem-Fachandi, *Pogrom in Gujarat* (Princeton, N.J.: Princeton University Press, 2012), 26.

2. Constructing the Proto-Terrorist

I WAS DRAFTING THIS BOOK, in May 2022, when news broke out about the death of fourteen-year-old Rezwan Kohistani. Rezwan had been found dead, hanging from a tree in a field behind Webb City High School in Missouri. He had arrived in Missouri with his family just four months earlier, fleeing the Taliban takeover of Afghanistan that was precipitated by the withdrawal of American armed forces from the country in 2021. His father had spent years distributing fuel to Americans and was able to catch an overcrowded flight arranged as part of American rescue effort.[1] The family was resettled in the rural town of Oronogo by a government subcontractor. Oronogo, according to U.S. census data, is over 90 percent white.[2] There were no Afghan families for miles.[3] Rezwan's school had never enrolled a refugee before; it did not have any Dari translators on staff.

The Missouri chapter of the Council on American-Islamic Relations, a Muslim civil rights watchdog, issued a statement suggesting that Rezwan had been subjected to anti-Muslim and

1. Kartikay Mehrotra and Matti Gellman, "What Happened to Rezwan," *ProPublica*, November 19, 2022, https://www.propublica.org /article/missouri-afghan-refugees-rezwan-kohistani-oronogo.
2. U.S. Census, data from July 2021, https://www.census.gov /quickfacts/webbcitycitymissouri (accessed May 22, 2022).
3. Mehrotra and Gellman, "What Happened to Rezwan."

racist bullying. The school denied those claims. The county coroner initially ruled his death a suicide by hanging, though he later abstained from reiterating that in the final report, saying that the investigation was ongoing. The reaction on Twitter to the initial ruling was scathing. As @Sammerstein put it, "People of color do not commit suicide by hanging themselves from trees."[4] When another Twitter user questioned @Sammerstein's interpretation, she elaborated: "Bc that's how lynchings get covered up in this country historically. 100% mental health is not taken serious in this country and people need access but saying an outdoor hanging in a place he was extremely bullied [w]as a suicide with no further investigation is sus af."[5] Other commentators saw Rezwan's death as a lesson in intimidation. That is, of course, what a lynching is and does: beyond killing the targeted individual, it leaves behind a tortured body to remind a nonwhite public of its unbelonging. That in these social media posts the lens of lynching was used for a Brown body signals that anti-Black and anti-Brown violence in America can overlap in form and methods.

While we may not ever know for certain whether Rezwan's death was a suicide or a lynching—as of June 2023, the investigation was still ongoing[6]—there is good reason to believe that he was bullied for "contaminating" a predominantly white space. During Ramadan, his classmates made fun of him for not eating during lunch; he sometimes came home crying.[7] Teasing and bullying, in such a context, can imply an intention to exclude him from the social life of the community, and even from the community itself. Indeed, bullied kids often leave the schools where they have been made miserable; the teen suicides that result from bullying constitute a

4. Shrimp LOL mein (@Sammerstein), Twitter, May 20, 2022, 6:32 p.m. https://twitter.com/Sammerstein/status/1527779198617718787.

5. Shrimp LOL mein (@Sammerstein), Twitter, May 21, 2022, 2:51 p.m. https://twitter.com/Sammerstein/status/1528086022789136386.

6. Email communication, Matti Gellman, August 22, 2023.

7. Mehrotra and Gellman, "What Happened to Rezwan."

particularly tragic form of that leaving. And an actual lynching, if that was indeed Rezwan's fate, might thus be understood as a more violent and direct expression of exclusionary intent.

The question we must ask is: Why and how did a Muslim boy from Afghanistan arrive in a mostly white, rural town of Missouri in the first place? That people like Rezwan are now on American soil is directly linked to the long American war in Afghanistan, a war in which many working-class white American soldiers and servicemembers also died or were wounded. But instead of an alliance between rural Americans and Afghan refugees, we see misdirected rage and efforts to punish someone who is considered a threat to the dominant group. This tragic episode thus prompts us to think about how a long phase of U.S. military intervention in Muslim countries is both provoked by and then (unfairly) provokes U.S.-based anti-Muslim anger, and why and how that anger points to Muslim boys in particular. The warfare industry both needs and creates anti-Muslim sentiment. In an alternate reality we might see poor, white, rural families of soldiers and ex-soldiers perceiving themselves in the same boat as the refugees, as co-victims of the military-industrial complex. But capitalism works hard to achieve enmity between these two groups lest they join together against a system that actually injures both.

In this chapter, I begin by first situating Rezwan's experience in the context of American empire and elaborate on how foreign wars have reshaped notions of risk and threat within the U.S. I then turn my attention to two sites—educational institutions and national borders—to outline some of the discursive practices through which Muslim boys are conjured as "proto-terrorists," a figuration that helps fuel the American war economy.

American Warfare Capitalism

Afghan refugees are seeking asylum in the United States because they are fleeing the repercussions of a protracted U.S.-sponsored war in Afghanistan and past American decisions to fund extremist organizations in the country of their birth. Tens of thousands of Afghans—Rezwan's family among them—flowed out of Afghanistan in 2021 in direct and painful consequence of the trillions of U.S. dollars and the hundred thousand U.S. troops that formerly flooded in, largely to promote U.S. geopolitical interests. Back in the 1970s, America and Saudi Arabia funneled billions of dollars to the *mujahidin* (literally, those who engage in struggle) in Afghanistan to fight the Soviets. Most of these funds and weapons—and not coincidentally—went to groups that espoused extremist interpretations of Islam, as religious rigidity seemed a bulwark against communist ideology.[8] The ideology of jihad, described as holy war, was particularly instrumentalized and used by the United States and its allies to recruit Muslims across the world. After the Soviet Union withdrew from Afghanistan in 1989, civil war ensued among the Afghan factions; from that struggle eventually emerged the Afghan Taliban, who came to power in 1996 with U.S. support. U.S.-Afghan relations turned sour when the Taliban refused to hand over Osama bin Laden, who had established his base in Afghanistan and whom U.S. authorities deemed responsible for the 9/11 attacks. In 2001, the United States, together with NATO forces, began a military operation in Afghanistan that lasted two decades.

According to the Cost of War project at Brown University, the war wreaked havoc in Afghanistan: food insecurity increased from 62 percent (pre-2001) to 92 percent (in 2022), the percentage of children under five experiencing acute malnutrition increased from 9 percent to 50 percent, and the share of Afghans living in poverty increased from 80 percent to 97 percent. By the end of 2021, an estimated 4.3 million Afghans had been internally displaced. In 2022, there were 1.5 million Afghans living with disabilities (largely related to military action) and two million widows. The displacement and dispossession of Afghans was profitable for the United

8. Charles Hirschkind and Saba Mahmood, "Feminism, the Taliban, and Politics of Counter-Insurgency," *Anthropological Quarterly* 75, no. 2 (2002): 343.

States and its allies, for both public entities and private companies.[9] War economies thrive on new wars, which create jobs for the military and its contractors, fund new weapons projects, and are used to justify building new prisons. Of the fourteen trillion total dollars Pentagon spent on the war in Afghanistan, one-third to one-half went to military contractors, especially to U.S.-based weapons contractors (Lockheed Martin, Boeing, General Dynamics, Raytheon, and Northrop Grumman), which together received over $286 billion in contracts in 2019 and 2020 alone.[10] Over the twenty years of war in Afghanistan, other weapons manufacturers, logistics and reconstruction firms like KBR and Bechtel, and armed private security contractors like Blackwater and Dyncorp, also profited.[11]

U.S. mining interests were another under-discussed factor in the prolonged U.S. presence that ultimately upended Rezwan's life in Afghanistan. Whether commissioning exploratory surveys or pressuring the Afghan government to deliver access to foreign corporations, the United States was particularly interested in Afghanistan's mineral deposits: rare-earth minerals, lithium, and copper with a value estimated at one to three trillion dollars.[12] In 2017, Trump and Ghani agreed to mining contracts that gave beneficial treatment to U.S. companies.[13] While then U.S. Secretary of Commerce Wilbur

9. While many contractors pulled out with the military, some are still operating; see Lynzy Billing, "The U.S. Is Leaving Afghanistan? Tell That to the Contractors: American Firms Capitalize on the Withdrawal, Moving in with Hundreds of New Jobs," *New York Magazine*, May 12, 2021, https://nymag.com/intelligencer/2021/05/u-s-contractors-in-afghanistan-are-hiring-amid-withdrawal.html.

10. William Hartung, "Corporate Power, Profiteering, and the 'Camo Economy,'" *Watson Institute*, September 13, 2021, 4.

11. Hartung, 5.

12. William Byrd and Javed Noorani, "Exploitation of Mineral Resources in Afghanistan," *USIP Peace Brief*, December 1, 2014.

13. Special Inspector General for Afghanistan Reconstruction, *Quarterly Report to the U.S. Congress*, October 30, 2017; Antony Loewenstein, "Peace in Afghanistan? Maybe—but a Minerals Rush Is Already Underway," *The Nation*, January 30, 2019.

Ross used the language of development and self-reliance to discuss these mining ventures ("The whole idea of it is to try to figure out how to make Afghanistan a self-sufficient country that can provide jobs for its people and its own budget," he said), President Trump eyed the minerals as an opportunity to recoup U.S. spending on war: "As the prime minister of Afghanistan has promised, we are going to participate in economic development to help defray the cost of this war to us."[14]

When American troops exited in 2021, Afghanistan was again taken over by the Taliban. Of the thousands of Afghans who fled the country in its immediate aftermath only a limited number have been able to find asylum; others are still waiting. More than 76,000 Afghans were evacuated to the United States, but most were admitted under the humanitarian parole provision, a temporary protected status that allows them to work and live but bears an expiration date and does not lead to lawful permanent residence.[15] Afghans who received humanitarian parole have to apply for other forms of immigration or return to the country from where they came. The path

14. Quoted in Elias Groll, "Despite Risks, Trump Administration Moves Forward with Afghanistan Mining Plan," Foreign Policy, August 29, 2017, https://foreignpolicy.com/2017/08/29/despite-risks-trump-administration-moves-forward-with-afghanistan-mining-plan/. America is only one in a series of actors in a long history of extractive capitalism in Afghanistan; the Soviet Union eyed Afghanistan's minerals (and ports) in the past and, with America's own recent exit, China is now ready to step into the role of extractor.

15. Department of Homeland Security, "Operation Allies Welcome," Government of United States, https://www.dhs.gov/allieswelcome; U.S. Citizenship and Immigration Services, "Temporary Protected Status Designation: Afghanistan," Government of United States, https://www.uscis .gov/humanitarian/temporary-protected-status/temporary-protected-status -designated-country-afghanistan; International Rescue Committee, "Two Years On, Afghan Potential in U.S. Communities Hindered by Lack of Pathway to Permanent Status," press release, August 11, 2023, https://www.rescue .org/press-release/2-years-afghan-potential-us-communities-hindered -lack-pathway-permanent-status; Andorra Bruno, "Permanent Immigration Options for Afghans with Immigration Parole," Congressional Research Service, 2022, https://crsreports.congress.gov/product/pdf/R/R47165/1.

to full residency for these Afghans remains uncertain, lengthy, and difficult. In contrast, pathways such as refugee or special immigrant visas are supported by federal funds and lead to lawful residence. Afghan refugees struggle with everyday life challenges: they may not be able to speak English; they may experience bullying and other discrimination; they may be living in poverty.

The United States is thus now home not only to tens of thousands of military combat veterans who fought outside the United States in a War on Terror broadly conceptualized as foreign, but also to tens of thousands of refugees displaced from regions where the U.S. military brought its acts of war. Rezwan arrived in Missouri as the result of a war that can be linked directly to American intervention, war economies, and capitalist extraction. Displaced by U.S. sponsored state violence in places many of them used to call home, Muslim boys like Rezwan are now bullied, surveilled, and detained in the United States as an extension of this war activity. The impacts of American wars are thus not limited to territories and peoples outside America; they can be felt domestically as well.

Beyond the U.S. military intervention in Afghanistan, the broader "war on terror" has inaugurated many changes to domestic security—in particular, the collapse into each other of military and police authority, two manifestations of state-authorized violence that had previously been separated for use against threats either foreign or domestic. We see this conflation in a new dispensation of sharing between institutions like the FBI and the CIA, in the recycling of combat equipment from the military to local police forces, and in special programs that give local law-enforcement entities access to discounted federal prices on items like rifles, helicopters, and Mine-Resistant Ambush Protected vehicles.[16] This expansion of the security regime relies on the construction of an ongoing threat,

16. Michael Owens, Tom Clark, and Adam Glynn, "Where Do Police Departments Get Their Military-Style Gear?" *The Washington Post*, July 20, 2020, https://www.washingtonpost.com/politics/2020/07/20/where -do-police-departments-get-their-military-style-gear-heres-what-we-dont -know/.

which keeps America, in David Theo Goldberg's words, on a "permanent war footing."[17] It presumes, writes Goldberg, "that nations are now under constant attack from rogue forces, antistatists, quasi states, and terrorists . . . The projection of constant threat or possibility of violent events is taken to require not just vigilance but perpetual preparation."[18] The construction of threat and risk that have kept America on a permanent war footing is ultimately a domestic project. Some elements of this project are visible in American schools and at our borders.

Constructing the *Proto*-Terrorist

In 2016, a seven-year-old Muslim boy Abdul Aziz was kicked and punched in the aisle of his school bus as his classmates talked of him as Muslim and Pakistani; his older brothers in the past had been called "terrorists."[19] That same year when two Muslim teens were attacked outside a mosque in Brooklyn, their assailant reportedly shouted, "You f**king terrorist" and "You Muslims are the cause of all the problems of the world."[20] Pia Rebello Britto finds that the

17. Goldberg, "Militarizing Race," 21.

18. Goldberg, 21.

19. Chris Sommerfeldt, "Muslim Boy, 7, Beaten Onboard School Bus in North Carolina because of Donald Trump's Hateful Rhetoric: Father," *New York Daily News*, October 13, 2016, https://www.nydailynews.com /news/national/muslim-boy-7-beaten-classmates-trump-father-article-1 .2828749; Rachael Revesz, "Seven-Year-Old Muslim Schoolboy Abdul Aziz Speaks about Being Bullied on a School Bus," *Independent*, October 16, 2016, https://www.independent.co.uk/news/world/americas/abdul-aziz-usmani -video-watch-muslim-islamophobic-bully-school-bus-north-carolina -pakistan-a7362041.html.

20. Ben Yakas, "Two Muslim Teens Beaten Outside Brooklyn Mosque, Cops Don't Think It's a Hate Crime," *Gothamist*, July 5, 2016, https:// gothamist.com/news/two-muslim-teens-beaten-outside-brooklyn-mosque -cops-dont-think-its-a-hate-crime; Reuters Staff, "Two Muslim Teens Beaten outside New York Mosque: Rights Group," *Reuters*, July 4, 2016, https://www.reuters.com/article/us-new-york-muslims-attack/two-muslim -teens-beaten-outside-new-york-mosque-rights-group-idUSKCN0ZL01K.

years following 9/11 saw an increase in reports of discrimination, bullying, and exclusion of Arab Muslim children.[21] And in the incidents considered above we note the incessant marking of Muslim boys as "terrorists," a framing that is not applied to nonwhite boys as a group. Insults like "terrorist" and "Go back to where you came from," are speech acts through which that which threatens the self and identity is subjugated; and an illusion of purity, homogeneity, and integrity is reestablished.

The figure of the terrorist is made comprehensible in the West today through recourse to longstanding ideas about monstrosity: this association has been carefully explored by scholars including Sophia Arjana, Farzana Shain, Amit Rai, and Jasbir Puar.[22] Arjana meticulously examines the depiction of Muslims as monsters in medieval European literature; Shain highlights the trope of the folk devil as it has been applied to Muslim men in England since the mid-1980s; Rai and Puar draw on Foucault's discussion of abnormality to examine the construction of the Muslim terrorist-monster. These ideas about monstrosity are helpful in understanding the conceptualization of "terrorist" as a persona of adult Muslim men.[23]

21. Pia Rebello Britto, "Who Am I? Ethnic Identity Formation of Arab Muslim Children in Contemporary U.S. Society," *Journal of the American Academy of Child and Adolescent Psychiatry* 47, no. 8 (2008): 854.

22. Sophia Arjana, *Muslims in the Western Imagination* (Oxford: Oxford University Press, 2015); Jasbir Puar and Amit Rai, "Monster, Terrorist, Fag," *Social Text* 20, no. 3 (2002) 117–48; Farzana Shain, "Dangerous Radicals or Symbols of Crisis and Change," in *Muslim Students, Education, and Neoliberalism,* ed. Martin Mac an Ghaill and Chris Haywood (Basingstoke, UK: Palgrave Macmillan, 2017): 17–33. Deepa Kumar points out that the word 'terrorist' did not always connote Arab or South Asian Muslim men, the association developed over time as U.S. strategic ally Israel intensified its imperial ambitions in Gaza and the West Bank (Deepa Kumar, "Terrorcraft: Empire and the Making of the Racialized Terrorist Threat," *Race & Class* 62, no. 2 [2020]: 34).

23. Shenila Khoja-Moolji, "The Making of 'Humans' and their Others in/through Human Rights Advocacy," *Signs: Journal of Women in Culture and Society* 42, no. 2 (2017): 377–402.

But when we consider Muslim boys, two further "abnormal" figures identified by Foucault become useful: the individual to be corrected and the masturbating child.[24] Of the three figures Foucault uses to describe the domain of abnormality as it developed in the West during the eighteenth and nineteenth centuries—between medieval laws and the discourses of psychiatry—the monstrous may be least relevant to the construction of Muslim boyhood. Foucault considers the "individual to be corrected" in relation to discipline, and the "masturbating child" to understand how deviant behaviors come to be located in the body as pathology. As figures targeted for different forms of power, these archetypes may also help us understand how the modern system of correction and punishment comes into being.[25] Specifically, Foucault writes about the emergence of a new kind of psychiatric knowledge and its associated experts, whose purpose is not to cure patients but to provide testimony so that society can be protected from those patients. The psychiatrist thus appears in the courtroom, and the focus of testimony shifts from "crime committed (an actual crime) to crime that *could* be committed (potential crime)."[26] In this way, modern systems of correction and punishment bring together juridical and psychiatric discourses to punish infractions—and also to *predict* or *detect* them.

Foucault's framing is relevant to our discussion of Muslim boyhood because it helps us recognize the numerous disciplinary interventions aimed at Muslim boys as not simply corrective but as diagnostic, aimed at identifying the proto-terrorist and anticipating or thwarting crime before it happens. That is the framing proposed by Tom Ridge, appointed to lead the new Department of Homeland

24. Michel Foucault, *Abnormal Lectures at the College de France 1974–1975* (London: Verso, 2016).

25. Veena Das, *On reading Abnormal (1974–75)*, Columbia Blogs, November 10, 2015, https://blogs.law.columbia.edu/foucault1313/2015/11/10/foucault-513-veena-das-on-reading-abnormal-1974-75/.

26. Das.

Security created as part of the massive U.S. response to 9/11: "It's not a question of if, but when."[27] For someone like Ridge, who seems to "know" that a terror attack will take place on U.S. soil—and who sees himself as charged to prevent that attack—it's only a short conceptual step from *when* to *who*. In a world where terrorist proclivities are increasingly naturalized as pathologies and located in the body (as is described in Amit Rai and Jasbir Puar's work), boyhood becomes the developmental stage in which these pathologies are ideally detected. In other words, while Muslim men may be terrorists, Muslim boys are imagined as terrorists-in-the-making or proto-terrorists. This framing is politically useful as it makes tomorrow's terrorism visible today, albeit in an inchoate form. As Todd Ramlow notes, in order to defuse any threat to the social order presented by a cultural other, the threat must first be made visible:[28] visibility and manageability go together. The proto-terrorist concretizes threat by making it visible and thus creates an opportunity for the security regime to manage it. The state then enters the lives of Muslim boys through commensurate technologies of monitoring, surveillance, quarantine, suspension, and abandonment.

The construction, detection, and management of Muslim boys *as* proto-terrorists—where it is most readily differentiated from the management of Black and Brown youth more generally—can be seen in American educational institutions and at U.S. national borders. While prisons are a paradigmatic site of incarceration and slow death for Black youth and adult men, at the additional sites of schools and borders we gain insight into how nonwhite—and particularly Brown Muslim—bodies experience carcerality in ways that are both like and unlike the experiences of Black Muslims or U.S. Black populations in general. At check-in, TSA screening, and customs lines at airports, and in detention rooms

27. As cited in Katharyne Mitchell, "Pre-Black Futures," *Antipode* 41, no. 1 (2010): 241.

28. Todd Ramlow, "Bad Boys: Abstracts of Difference and the Politics of Youth 'Deviance,'" *GLQ* 9, no. 1–2 (2003): 201.

and surveillance programs implemented at schools and colleges, we see additional acts of enclosure that particularly target Brown Muslim populations.

Monitoring the "Leakage" at Schools

The FBI describes its involvement in schools as part of a broader strategy to address violent extremism via local partnerships. The rather surprising idea that a federal agency dedicated to the investigation of complex crimes has a reason to speak directly to U.S. middle and high schools should be read against the many changes to domestic security inaugurated by the War on Terror. In a 2010 national security strategy, such involvements were deemed a key "defense" against "the threat to the United States":

> Several recent incidences of violent extremists in the United States who are committed to fighting here and abroad have underscored the threat to the United States and our interests posed by individuals radicalized at home. Our best defenses against this threat are well informed and equipped families, local communities, and institutions. The Federal Government will invest in intelligence to understand this threat and expand community engagement and development programs to empower local communities.[29]

A 2011 White House report, "Empowering Local Partners to Prevent Violent Extremism in the United States," follows up with particular interest in schools and youth agencies. Staff at these entities can "help identify causes, recommend appropriate responses, and select activities for local implementation."[30] The terms "threat," "threats," and "threatening" appear nineteen times in this eight-page document, and while domestic extremists and hate crimes are mentioned, the document's repeated mentions of al-Qa'ida make clear where the authors see that "threat" most concretely located.

29. National Security Strategy, May 2010 cited in The White House, *Empowering Local Partners to Prevent Violent Extremism in the United States,* Government of United States, August 2011, 1.

30. The White House, 4.

From the existence of a general threat, the report turns its attention to Muslims, who may surveil their communities on behalf of the state: "Communities—especially Muslim American communities whose children, families, and neighbors are being targeted for recruitment by al-Qa'ida—are often best positioned to take the lead because they know their communities best."[31] Even while asking communities to monitor the behavior of their own youth, law enforcement agencies view outreach to schools as a key aspect of community policing strategy. In a federally funded 2014 survey of U.S. law enforcement agencies (whose combined jurisdictions covered eighty-six percent of the U.S. population), 45.2 percent of the agencies described presentations at schools as a commonly used community policing strategy.[32]

The FBI sees school personnel as key agents for identifying "catalysts that drive violent extremism"—an opportunity to enlist school staff as observers of a surveilled student population, and specifically of students who belong to risk groups.[33] The 2016 FBI report "Preventing Violent Extremism in Schools" asks teachers, social workers, and school administrators to monitor students and report to law enforcement about any students deemed risky. This report on "extremism prevention" emphasizes adolescence as a chaotic developmental stage during which young people are "more susceptible to embracing violent extremist ideologies" and are prone to being influenced by underlying "risk factors" (such as family dynamics) and external stimuli (indoctrination).[34] The FBI's focus on unstable family dynamics and developmental stages is in line with a broader consensus within the field of terrorism studies

31. The White House, preface.
32. David Schanzer, Charles Kurzman, Jessica Toliver, and Elizabeth Miller, *The Challenge and Promise of Using Community Policing Strategies to Prevent Violent Extremism*, Triangle Center on Terrorism and Homeland Security, 2016.
33. FBI, *Preventing Violent Extremism in Schools*, Office of Partner Engagement, January 2016, 1.
34. FBI, 7.

that childhood circumstances are a crucial determining factor in whether an individual will be susceptible to recruitment into terrorist activities. As Rai and Puar have explained, terrorism experts often seek to uncover foundational moments in the construction of the terrorist psyche.[35] The terrorist is assumed to have personality defects rooted in childhood experiences within the family—the individual may have grown up in a dysfunctional family, or might conversely rebel against society out of loyalty to parents perceived as injured.[36] With terrorist proclivities lodged in his psyche, the proto-terrorist is an individual who, although he has not yet committed a crime, is certain to do so; he must therefore be monitored, not in the expectation that he might be educated or reformed out of his (inevitable) wrongdoing, but that he might be caught before the crime. Childhood and adolescence, as we see in the FBI report, thus come under intense scrutiny.

Having located terrorist proclivities in a youth's or student's psyche, the 2016 report further attempts to identify everyday practices that might hint at *future* criminal behavior. The FBI describes these as "leakage" or "common warning behavior for students advocating violence," in an explicit reference to anticipated acts: "Leakage occurs when a student intentionally or unintentionally reveals clues to feelings, thoughts, fantasies, attitudes, or intentions that signal an impending act. These clues emerge as subtle threats, boasts, innuendos, predictions, or ultimatums and are conveyed in numerous forms (e.g. stories, diaries, journals, essays, poems, manifestos, letters, songs, drawings, and videos)."[37] The long list of media and forms of expression that the report suggests can furnish insights into young people's thoughts gives tacit permission to school personnel to monitor children's activities in this broad range of contexts where

35. Puar and Rai, "Monster, Terrorist, Fag," 122.

36. Charles Ruby cited in Amit Rai, "Of Monsters," *Cultural Studies* 18, no. 4 (2004): 545.

37. FBI, *Preventing Violent Extremism in Schools*, 17.

"leakage" might happen—and where monitoring can thus detect future terrorism (or in the FBI's language, "an impending act").[38]

That teachers are asked to always be on the lookout for "leakage" or signs of criminality in students' homework assignments, stated comments and opinions, or online activity helps to explain in part why Ahmed Mohamed's English teacher thought that his home-made clock was a bomb. Popular culture could also be a driving factor. Television shows such as Homeland liberally feature the Islamic-figure-with-a-bomb-in-U.S.-domestic-setting scaremon-gering. Some of the pressure on teachers to watch out for "leak-age" also comes from school shootings (most often perpetrated by someone inside the school, not usually for political reasons). Having reached—or leaped to—that conclusion, Ahmed's teacher followed school and district procedure of informing the school principal and law enforcement, who hold the authority to bring the suspected student inside the carceral system. As the FBI report instructs, "Students and educators are encouraged to convey their concerns and observations to trusted community partners, school resource of-ficers, or a local law enforcement entity."[39] The FBI has also reached out to students directly to enroll them in this endeavor. In 2016, it launched an interactive website aimed at teens—"Don't Be a Puppet: Pull Back the Curtain on Violent Extremism"—that features colorful graphics, quizzes, videos, activities, and other materials "to teach teens how to recognize violent extremist messaging and become more resistant to self-radicalization and possible recruitment."[40] Students are thus encouraged to view their classmates with suspi-cion and participate in this project of surveillance.

38. The FBI is not alone in enlisting teachers to monitor Muslim students; the United Kingdom's Prevent program similarly calls on teachers and administrative staff to monitor students and refer them to the govern-ment's anti-radicalization program (Department for Education, *The Prevent Duty,* Government of United Kingdom, June 2015, 4).

39. FBI, *Preventing Violent Extremism in Schools,* 22.

40. FBI, "FBI Launches New Awareness Program for Teens," February 8, 2016, https://www.fbi.gov/news/stories/countering-violent-extremism.

Yet, the Muslim boy thus identified does not become Foucault's "individual to be corrected." He remains outside the system's capacity to reform; his path to correction is not via education, but rather through expulsion and quarantine. Ahmed, for instance, was first questioned by the school principal and police officers in a closed room and then taken to a juvenile detention facility in handcuffs, where he was fingerprinted and interrogated without his parents present. He was eventually suspended from school for three days. Muslim boys, as proto-terrorists, lack the complexity of "at-risk" figures (who might be reformed) and are instead what Katharyne Mitchell terms as "pre-known risk failure[s]."[41] While Mitchell writes about Black boys in particular, we can extend this framing to Muslim boys as well: instead of "at risk," Muslim boys are "a risk."

The search for "leakage" frequently manifests as bullying. In 2016, the American Civil Liberties Union filed a complaint with the Department of Justice requesting an investigation of Faye Myles, a teacher at a charter school in Phoenix, Arizona. The ACLU alleged Myles had repeatedly singled out, abused, and even physically assaulted a Muslim boy, A.A., then eleven years old and in the sixth grade. According to the complaint, Myles choked A.A. and then intimidated him into hiding the incident from his parents: "If you tell your mom, watch what happens next."[42] A.A. did inform his mother, who complained to the school, but Myles denied choking A.A. and the school reported that it had uncovered no wrongdoing. In the months following the alleged attack, Myles allegedly taunted A.A., even imagining him into the figure of proto-terrorist. After showing a video clip of events related to September 11, 2001, she told A.A., "That's going to be you." The complaint further de-

41. Mitchell, "Pre-Black Futures." On Black boyhood in America see Michael Dumas and Joseph Nelson, "(Re)Imagining Black Boyhood," *Harvard Educational Review* 86, no. 1 (2016): 27–47.

42. As cited in American Civil Liberties Union, "Noor Complaint to the Department of Justice Requesting an Investigation Pursuant to Title IV," October 28, 2016.

scribes a sweeping condemnation from Myles, in a moment when A.A. wanted to answer a question she had posed to the class: "All you Muslims think you are so smart . . . I can't wait until Trump is elected. He's going to deport all you Muslims. Muslims shouldn't be given visas. They'll probably take away your visa and deport you. You're going to be the next terrorist, I bet."[43] These comments reiterate the close association between Muslimness and boyhood as a sign of future crime ("that's going to be you" and "You're going to be the next terrorist") that I have been discussing thus far. Also worth noting is the teacher's intuitive reference to borders and assumption of border security officers' broad power to monitor and expel Muslim boys ("They'll probably take away your visa and deport you"). That the bullying legitimized at school can spill over to other sites is evident in A.A.'s later harassment on the school bus by his peers, who had heard him shamed in the classroom, and now proceeded to call him a "terrorist."[44]

"Leakage" and Imputed Abnormality

The proto-terrorist "leakage" that the FBI wants schools and community organizations to detect is ascribed by some psychologists and social workers to supposed abnormal sexual and emotional development among Muslim boys—an imputed abnormality that, in turn, purportedly manifests in rage and violence in adulthood. Foucault's formulation of the masturbating child is thus a persuasive model for understanding how Muslim boys are pathologized: terrorist proclivities are lodged in their bodies. And, while all Muslim boys are constructed as proto-terrorists, family circumstances may render certain boys at greater risk of leaking or expressing the proto-terrorist nature that this "logic" would impose on them as a group.

Consider a mental health screening framework developed by psychologists Cyrus Ho, Tian Quek, Roger Ho, and Carol Choo. It

43. American Civil Liberties Union.
44. American Civil Liberties Union.

focuses particular attention on social factors to identify patients at high risk for being involved in terrorist activity: "Family dysfunction; Friendship with radicalized individuals; Living in, or with close links to, an unstable geopolitical area; Unemployment or underemployment; *No history of romantic relationships*" (emphasis added).[45] The suggestion that sexual frustration—an individual has not experienced proper sexual milestones—is a predictor for terrorist behavior echoes as a broader social trope in discussions of young Muslim men. Thus David Frum, former speechwriter for George W. Bush, could remark on the first anniversary of the 9/11 attacks, "The Middle East is now a region of overpopulation and underemployment, where tens of millions of young men waste their lives in economic and sexual frustration."[46] Frum, as we shall see below, relies on specific Western stereotypes to assume the sexual frustration of young Muslim men in the Middle East and then uses that to explain their expected violence. A pattern of sexual rejection has been seen to have fueled a number of mass shootings by young white men,[47] but when talking about Muslim boys, observers like Frum do not describe instances of individual psychological development or lack (as we would typically see emerge in conversations around mass shootings by white non-Muslim men). Instead, they project sexual frustration onto an entire cohort based on a Western interpretation of the social effects of growing up in an Islamic culture. As Amit Rai observes, biographical accounts of terrorists written by

45. Cyrus Ho, Tian Quek, Roger Ho, and Carol Choo, "Terrorism and Mental Illness: A Pragmatic Approach for the Clinician," *BJPsych Advances* 25 (2019): 101–9.

46. David Frum, "The Truth," *American Enterprise Institute*, October 25, 2002, https://www.aei.org/articles/the-truth/. See Caluya, "Sexual Geopolitics," on the conflation of sexual frustration and economic deprivation as the explanation for international terrorism (Gilbert Caluya, "Sexual Geopolitics: The 'Blue Balls' Theory of Terrorism," *Continuum 27*, no. 1 [2013]: 54–66).

47. Kate Manne, *Down Girl: The Logic of Misogyny* (New York: Oxford University Press, 2018).

Western journalists similarly focus on deviations from presumably normal childhoods that lead to later sexual frustration or excesses.[48] Journalist Adam Robinson presents Osama bin Laden as a normal child until his father's death, after which he loses himself in "hedonistic pleasures":

> The only son of a mother who immediately fell out of favor with his father; the urge to please, to impress, to be accepted were driving forces in his childhood. His father's death when he was ten years old seems to have unhinged him and, from then on, he swung crazily like an ever-more dangerous wrecker's ball from one obsessive attachment to another. At first, the only person he damaged was himself: living in the world of books, he cut himself off from the world that his brothers and sisters inhabited. Then he swung in the opposite direction, losing himself in hedonistic pleasures abroad as only one with unlimited funds can do.[49]

In this framing we see not only a troubled childhood marked by one parent's outsider status and the death of the other, but also an aberrant sexuality—here denoted by "hedonistic pleasures," differently aberrant to the "no history of romantic relationships" we see on the list of terrorism social risk factors above and yet similarly linking terrorism and sexual frustration.

Young Muslim men as a group, then, are either sexually deprived or oversexed. This contradictory knowledge ultimately turns the subject into someone who is incapable of managing personal emotions and desires, sexual or otherwise. The binary framing in turn relies on the dual depiction of Muslim societies in the Western imaginary: on the one hand, Muslim societies are marked by polygamy (harnessing fantasies about men who have unrestrained access to women); on the other hand, images of all-male madrasas evoke imaginings of a gender-segregated Muslim society where men grow up in homosocial spaces, with few or limited encounters with women. These contradictory conceptualizations—sexual over-

48. Rai, "Of Monster," 546.
49. Robinson as cited in Rai, 546.

indulgence/unrestrained access to women and sexual frustration/ no access to women—defy reconciliation, although their parallel existence is politically useful. Depending on the circumstances and audience, each can be mobilized to evoke politically powerful fears.

The Polish magazine *wSieci* panders to these fears in its 2016 cover story on the "Islamic Rape of Europe" (Figure 1): white, blond, female Europe, draped in the flag of the European Union, is terrified at being groped by brown, hairy arms. The image's tight cropping invites the viewer to imagine outside its frame oversexed/sexed-deprived migrant Muslim men who view women simply as vessels for their pleasure, to be discarded upon use. The underlying assumption here is that white, secular men will respect sexual boundaries, while Muslim men will not; that they will be unable to control their sexual appetites as the result of childhoods characterized by an "abnormality" that is framed as both familial and religious.

The idea that Muslim men threaten the sexual chastity of white women is widespread, and appears in the American context as well. In a 2017 interview, a suspect who had attacked a Muslim cab driver in Minnesota justified his assault by saying: "You tell me, do you not know what these Muslims will do with a white American girl?"[50] Likewise, on a recent visit to Atlanta, during a conversation about a different research project, I learned about the entrapment of a young Muslim man by the police in a case that again assumes deviant desires. The incident was relayed to me by his friend:

> So, I know this guy, twenty-year-old, a new migrant from Pakistan. He joined a chat channel or whatever and met a girl there. They decided to meet. When he got to the diner, she turned out to be a cop! Can you imagine that? He was arrested because the girl said she was seventeen or something. Like the cop who was being the girl. The dude from Pakistan didn't know anything about age laws probably. So he was arrested. He is in jail now. The lawyer told him to confess. He is in jail for one year. Can you imagine that?

50. New America, *Anti-Muslim Activities in the United States 2012–2018*, https://www.newamerica.org/in-depth/anti-muslim-activity/.

Figure 1. *wSieci* magazine cover, "Islamic Rape of Europe," 2016.

The young man's surprise at this entrapment was exacerbated by the fact that: "She had contacted him. Like, I mean, the cop had contacted him. So that's just messed up. Why would you do that to a poor guy? He is now withering away in jail." The police in this story seem to have enticed the young Pakistani man based on the expectation that he would be looking to prey on underage girls.

Catching Muslims boys *before* they commit a crime thus becomes an imperative for both state actors and proxies—teachers, fellow students, and even ordinary citizens. The New York Metropolitan Transportation Authority's "If You See Something, Say Something" campaign, launched in the aftermath of the September 11 attacks and transformed into a nationwide anti-terrorism movement by Department of Homeland Security in 2010, turns every citizen into someone who should engage in surveillance on behalf of the state.[51]

Surveillance as a Mobile Penitentiary

Explaining terrorism via individual pathology focuses attention on childhood experiences and hides the political reality that terrorism may well be driven by state and capitalist interests. It presents disciplinary and surveillance regimes such as the FBI's Preventing Violent Extremism program as ideal modes of intervention, while ignoring their racial prejudice. An administrative technique like watching out for "leakage," when directed against an at-risk/risk population that is numerically dominated by people who are Black and Brown, becomes another form of racial violence, no matter how loudly that technique is proclaimed to be routine or race-neutral. Entering the geography of the school can be a demoralizing experience for nonwhite students who are targeted daily for these surveillance procedures. And while nonwhite students from a range of backgrounds may perceive such monitoring and surveillance in largely similar ways, association with Muslimness—signified in the Western imagination by dress, accents, immigration status, or Brownness—means that Muslim boys (and girls) are enclosed by schools in ways that other students are not. Educator and community organizer Debbie Almontaser describes the significant anxiety over surveillance that she has observed among some Muslim high school students, and suggests that they may feel even worse if they knew its true extent:

> I spoke to high school juniors and seniors and [the issue of surveillance] came up. I asked them what they've been paying attention to politically. One of the kids said "NYPD spying." Another asked me do I think they're spying on us in school? I didn't want to freak the

51. Department of Homeland Security, "About the Campaign: 'If You See Something, Say Something®' Program," https://www.dhs.gov/see -something-say-something/about-campaign.

kids out, but the NYPD (via NYPD School Safety Agents) has access to surveillance cameras installed by the DOE (Department of Education) within the last several years inside middle and high school buildings. Live footage can be viewed from DOE Borough Centers.[52]

Schools are where many boys routinely encounter the carceral state. Thus, members of the focus groups I conducted in New York in 2017 to discuss the arrest of Ahmed Mohamed often moved rapidly from his encounter with the police to their own experiences with metal detectors and school safety officers. One participant described how routine surveillance can collide with bias:

> Whenever anything goes off—like if I am walking through scanning, as soon as I walk through scanning here [at school], let's say I have a simple penny—they are like instantly like, I heard one officer go 'just search him.' And they were like doing me like way more, more so because of, maybe the jacket or something. It was a lot more, more intense than if they were like checking someone else . . . I even took out the penny and offered to walk back in to just show it was a penny but they were like "no."

While female students are also disciplined, boys cited the comparative fragility of girls' bodies to explain why authorities saw them as less capable of participating in or enduring violence. When I asked my focus group participants about what might have happened if a girl, not a boy, had brought the homemade alarm clock to school, they said, "They would have been more soft on her. They probably would not have arrested her . . ." and "They would have been more lenient. She would have had more chances to explain herself." Nadir agreed with this view: "It would have been less . . . usually they fear that boys would do something and not females. So, they like they put them at different levels basically. If a boy did it, obviously, they would be scared because of how they perceive it . . . they perceive boys as harmful and harsh and stuff. And they perceive females as

52. As cited in Diala Shamas and Nermeen Arastu, *Mapping Muslims: NYPD Spying and its Impact on American Muslims* (Creating Law Enforcement Accountability and Responsibility Project, 2013), 45.

kind and calm and not like they would do anything like that." Riaz suggested further that gender shielded girls: "Girls are treated [a] little more sensitive[ly] because of the feminist movements that are going on right now. They would not really want to attack her because that would be the first thing people will bring up besides race." Imtiaz's comments similarly hint at the ways that gender stereotypes shape nonwhite boys' experiences in a society that adopts surveillance as a tool: "Sometimes your masculinity poses as a threat to others . . . so like, people look at men, some people do, as strong gender and they automatically think we will attack, do violence, like make bombs, use weapons than females . . ."

The boys in my group interview recognized, however, that race complicates this otherwise clear script of how girls experience school surveillance and its related discipline. Saleh saw room for a differentiated response, depending on the specific attributes of the hypothetical clock-making girl: "I think it depends on what the girl looks like. Like if she looked like a nice schoolgirl, like a skirt, and a white, like Catholic schoolgirl [everyone laughs] . . ." When Saleh invokes the stereotype of Catholic schoolgirls, he equates "nice" with being white, blond, and female. Such remarks are reminiscent of the broader cultural equivalence of whiteness and blondness with innocence, as we also saw in the *BBC News* coverage of Ukrainian refugees in chapter 1. Even schools that intentionally seek to create a welcoming and inclusive environment for immigrant students, according to Roozbeh Shirazi's study, end up making it contingent on them affirming white indigeneity, upholding the superiority of the United States, and limiting conversations about structural racism.[53] It is unsurprising then that many of my high school interlocutors felt that a nonwhite girl would not experience the same softness and forgiveness as a white girl.

---

53. Roozbeh Shirazi, "Between Hosts and Guests: Conditional Hospitality and Citizenship in an American Suburban School," *Curriculum Inquiry* 48, no. 1 (2018): 95–114.

In fact, across all five focus groups, my participants agreed that a girl who was visibly similar to Ahmed in race and religion (signified by the hijab) would likely undergo the same treatment—or even worse. One of my interlocutors suggested that it is probably because law officials assume that the girl would lead them to the real terrorists. In this framing, while girls' stronger visual association with Islam means that stereotypes associating Islam with terrorist violence could attach more powerfully to them, it is still boys/men who are considered the actual perpetrators or perpetrators-in-development. The interrogation of girls becomes a means to an end.[54]

The monitoring and surveillance of Muslim students is, if anything, intensified when they go to college. In 2001, the New York Police Department (NYPD) began a Muslim Surveillance and Mapping Program, which would continue until 2014. The NYPD sent informants to gather information in mosques, Muslim student groups, and Muslim-owned businesses in New York City and in nearby states. Included in this surveillance were thirty-one Muslim student associations (MSAs) on college campuses, of which seven were labeled "MSAs of concern." These included MSAs at Baruch College, Hunter College, La Guardia Community College, City College, Brooklyn College, St. John's University, and Queens College. According to the Creating Law Enforcement Accountability and Responsibility project at CUNY School of Law, NYPD also went into high schools and had a list of private Islamic schools "of interest."[55] The effect of this kind of close and sustained surveillance on Muslim communities can be devastating, constricting

54. We see similar dynamics unfold in the case of Naureen Laghari from Pakistan, a girl who was arrested in relation to a terror attack and later released. It was said that she was tricked by the real (male) terrorists. She was asked by the state to give lectures and appear on television to share her story with other youth to caution them against terrorist recruitment. See Shenila Khoja-Moolji, *Sovereign Attachments: Masculinity, Muslimness, and Affective Politics in Pakistan* (Oakland: University of California Press, 2021).

55. Shamas and Arastu, *Mapping Muslims*.

life and social relations. We can, in fact, see surveillance as a form of enclosure—and its life-stifling impacts as potentially analogous to those of the prison (as a recognized site of Black slow death).[56] This feeling of constriction is palpable in Asad Dandia's reflections on being targeted by an NYPD informant connected to its Muslim surveillance program.

In 2012 Dandia, then nineteen years old and studying at a community college in Brooklyn, was befriended by a young man over Facebook who wanted to get involved in Dandia's community-based charitable work. Dandia introduced him to colleagues and even invited him home for a meal. The young man later revealed himself to be an informant for the NYPD. Dandia was placed under surveillance because of his charitable work through an organization called Fesabeelillah Services of NYC, dedicated to serving low-income Muslims and non-Muslims alike. When the news of NYPD surveillance broke out in the media, it created intense confusion and mistrust among Muslims. Dandia recalls: "Mosques became even more anxious that newcomers were sent by the police. A chill swept through cafes and other businesses. Nobody knew whom to trust and people grew more afraid to voice their views openly. The world felt like it was closing in on us—because it was."[57] The feeling of lacking freedom, of being locked-in, is evident in Dandia's comments. He also worried about the borders, another site where surveillance and constriction are acutely felt. Dandia writes: "My mother wants to visit family in Pakistan this year, yet I'm afraid of what she might face at the airport . . . I, too, am scared to travel

---

56. Lauren Berlant uses 'slow death' in *Cruel Optimism* (Durham, N.C.: Duke University Press, 2011) to refer "to the physical wearing out of a population in a way that points to its deterioration as a defining condition of its experience and historical existence" (95).

57. Asad Dandia, "I Was a Muslim Teen under NYPD Surveillance. But Now I Have More Hope Than Ever," *ACLU Commentary*, March 7, 2017, https://www.aclu.org/news/national-security/i-was-muslim-teen-under-nypd-surveillance-now-i-have.

internationally—could I one day be refused reentry into the country of my birth?"[58] As we learned from the five-year-old Muslim boy's experience at Dulles, Dandia's trepidations were not without merit.

Suspension and Abandonment at the Borders

Returning to Sean Spicer's attempt to justify arresting a five-year-old Muslim boy at Dulles—"To assume that just because of someone's age and gender that they don't pose a threat would be misguided and wrong"—we can now appreciate his statement in new light: it is both constituted by, and constitutes, ideas about Muslim boys as proto-terrorists. When Donald Trump became president in 2017, one of his first acts was to issue executive order (EO 13769) "Protecting the Nation from Foreign Terrorist Entry into the United States." It was in the context of this order—which imposed a ninety-day ban restricting foreign nationals from seven predominantly Muslim countries from visiting the United States, suspended entry of all Syrian refugees indefinitely, and prohibited any other refugees from coming into the country for 120 days—that the five-year-old boy ended up detained in a Washington airport.

The ban was a reminder of older widely supported exclusionary laws, such as the Chinese Exclusion Act of 1882, which banned Chinese laborers from migrating to the United States on the grounds that they "endanger the good order of certain localities"[59] and the 1917 Barred Zone Act, which prevented Asian immigration altogether. Immigration restrictions were reduced significantly from the 1960s onward. But Trump's ban signaled a reversal. Even as the ACLU and the Council on American-Islamic Relations challenged Trump's 2017 executive order in court, the order received support, particularly among white evangelical Protestants, according to a

58. Dandia, "I Was a Muslim Teen."
59. Chinese Exclusion Act (1882).

study by the Pew Research Center.[60] While Joe Biden ended the ban in January 2021, Donald Trump started off his 2024 presidential primary campaign with claims that if reelected he would reinstate and increase the scope of the travel ban. In a statement made before a predominantly white audience in Council Bluffs, Iowa, Trump said: "When I return to office, the travel ban is coming back even bigger than before and much stronger than before. We don't want people blowing up our shopping centers."[61] In this ideological project, the five-year-old boy at Dulles is a harbinger of the adult man who blows up shopping centers.

The presence or risk of violence determines how a structure that at first glance is undifferentiated—in this case, a border zone—can be experienced differently by differently coded bodies. Helga Tawil-Souri reminds us that the experience and temporality of the border is subjective.[62] Racially marked bodies experience a given border space as difficult, slow, and unpredictable; in contrast, white bodies experience the same spacetime as rapid and predictable.[63] In international airports and other points of entry, the carceral practices of surveillance expand to contain and enclose nonwhite bod-

60. Gregory Smith, "Most White Evangelicals Approve of Trump Travel Prohibition and Express Concerns about Extremism," *Pew Research Center*, February 27, 2017, https://www.pewresearch.org/short-reads/2017/02/27/most-white-evangelicals-approve-of-trump-travel-prohibition-and-express-concerns-about-extremism/. For a detailed list of all court challenges see: https://www.aclu.org/other/lawsuits-related-trumps-muslim-ban.

61. Kathryn Watson and Zak Hudak, "Trump Says He'd Bring Back 'Travel Ban' That's 'Even Bigger than Before,'" *CBS News*, July 7, 2023, https://www.cbsnews.com/news/trump-bring-back-travel-ban-muslim-countries/.

62. Helga Tawil-Souri, 'Checkpoint Time,' *Qui parle* 26, no. 2 (2017): 383–422.

63. Ariel Handel, "Where, Where to, and When in the Occupied Territories: An Introduction to Geography of Disaster," in *The Power of Inclusive Exclusion: Anatomy of Israeli Rule in the Occupied Palestinian Territories,* ed. Adi Ophir, Michal Givoni, and Sari Hanafi (New York: Zone Books, 2009), 179–222.

ies in a liminal experience of permission to enter. Here, nonwhite bodies encounter state violence through proxies such as customs and patrol agents. Saher Selod argues that the "random" selection of people of color for searches and stops during state-led screening initiatives in airports in fact relies on "religious cues"—hijabs, beards, Arabic language, Muslim-sounding names—to determine who is a threat.[64] Fellow passengers, flight attendants, and pilots may also discriminate based on these same cues. Selod enumerates numerous instances of racialized surveillance: Muslim imams and women in hijab, and even a twelve-year-old Muslim boy, escorted off airplanes and interrogated, and released only after authorities determined they actually posed no threat.[65]

What stands out most in Selod's study of the experience of Muslims at airports is the indignity that they experience during pat-downs, stops, and searches, as these necessarily become public spectacles. Even though most of those stopped are soon released, the public performance of power is the point; it is through such performances that the state convinces onlookers of its own authority and necessity (as I have argued elsewhere in a discussion about state power).[66] Selod's interlocutors repeatedly shared feelings of humiliation, as did my interlocutors.[67] One of my focus group participants from Bangladesh recounted his father's harass-

64. Saher Selod, *Forever Suspect: Racialized Surveillance of Muslim Americans in the War on Terror* (Rutgers, N.J.: Rutgers University Press, 2018): 50.

65. Twelve-year-old Abdul, a Pakistani American Muslim, had his name placed on a (no-fly) list and consequently had difficulty boarding flights (Selod, *Forever Suspect,* 63). The watch lists created during the height of 9/11 are still in place twenty years later. See the experience of a Muslim leader from Seattle as documented in Nina Shapiro, "Muslim Imam in Seattle Sues over Mysterious FBI Watchlist," *Seattle Times,* August 13, 2023, https://www.seattletimes.com/seattle-news/law-justice/muslim -imam-in-seattle-sues-over-fbi-watchlist-that-never-ends/.

66. Selod, *Forever Suspect,* 67; Khoja-Moolji, *Sovereign Attachments.*

67. Compare the comments of my interlocutors to Saleem's experience in Selod, *Forever Suspect,* 61.

ment at the airport where he was held back for hours (more in chapter 4). Another young man recalled his experience at an airport security checkpoint: "[The agent] was super aggressive for no reason. I felt violated. I was shaking for hours after that incident." It is not surprising that, when possible, young Muslim men often prefer taking buses, which means enduring the inconvenience of a long, difficult trip in order to avoid the routinized surveillance of U.S. airports.[68]

Even the well-documented migrant crisis at the southwestern U.S. border—though its impacts are felt most powerfully by people migrating north from Mexico and Central America and which we don't ordinarily think about in relation to Muslims—has intensified partly due to the militarization of U.S. immigration policy in the wake of 9/11.[69] Longstanding prejudice against Latinx people is being shaped by new rumors about Muslim terrorists in South America to justify harsher treatment of Latinx migrants. Rumors have circulated that ISIS was setting up terror cells in Mexico, and in January 2019 Trump tweeted that a border rancher had found prayer rugs in New Mexico.[70] The fear of Muslims and associating Latinx border-crossers with Islam appears to be an effective tool for gaining public support around even harsher treatment of those migrants and asylum seekers. Indeed, during the Trump administration the United States saw a vast expansion in the detention of children at the borders. According to the Marshall Project, the U.S. Customs and Border Protection carried out thousands of child detentions a day, a total of almost half a million between

68. Anwar describes this preference for buses in Selod, *Forever Suspect*, 62.

69. Nazia Kazi, *Islamophobia, Race, and Global Politics* (Blue Ridge Summit, Pa.: Rowman and Littlefield Publishers, 2021).

70. See archived tweet at Aaron Rupar, "Trump's Unfounded Tweet Stoking Fears about Muslim 'Prayer Rugs,' Explained," *Vox News*, January 18, 2019, https://www.vox.com/2019/1/18/18188476/trump-muslim-prayer-rugs-tweet-border.

2016 and 2020.[71] A 2019 report from the Department of Homeland Security's internal watchdog noted "dangerous overcrowding and prolonged detention of children and adults in the Rio Grande Valley."[72] Rampant abuse by Customs and Border Protection officers, Border Patrol agents, and Immigration and Customs Enforcement officials has been reported for over a decade now.[73] Thus, even though the migrant crisis at the southwestern U.S. border might at first glance appear to be distinct from the discourse of terrorism linked to the Muslim ban, it is nonetheless connected when we recognize it as yet another manifestation of xenophobia that has long marked the Muslim condition in the United States.

In fact, in the last few years the southwestern border has become an entry point for increasing numbers of Muslims as they flee wars in the Middle East and Central Asia, as well as Russian military conscription. Even then Muslims make up less than 5 percent of border crossers. However, an investigation by *LA Times* revealed that for an eighteen-month period beginning in October 2021, 60 percent of those who were prosecuted by the U.S. attorney's office in Del Rio (under the failure-to-report law) were from Muslim-majority countries, including Afghanistan, Syria, Iran, and Mali.[74] Such a disproportionate state response should be by now as unsurprising to my readers as it is regrettable.

71. Anna Flagg and Andrew Calderon, "500,000 Kids, 30 Million Hours," *The Marshall Project*, October 30, 2020.

72. Office of Inspector General, *Management Alert—DHS Needs to Address Dangerous Overcrowding and Prolonged Detention of Children and Adults in the Rio Grande Valley (Redacted)*, July 2, 2019.

73. A. C. Thompson, "Over 200 Allegations of Abuse of Migrant Children," *Propublica*, May 31, 2019, https://www.propublica.org/article /over-200-allegations-of-abuse-of-migrant-children-1-case-of-homeland -security-disciplining-someone; John Shattuck, Sushma Raman, and Mathias Risse, *Holding Together: The Hijacking of Rights in America and How to Reclaim Them for Everyone* (New York: The New Press, 2022).

74. Hamed Aleaziz, "Asylum Seekers from Muslim-Majority Countries," *LA Times*, August 31, 2023, https://www.latimes.com/world -nation/story/2023-08-31/texas-prosecutions-muslim-asylum-seekers-1459.

Enclosing the Muslim Boy

In outlining the different discursive regimes within which Muslim boyhood takes shape, this chapter has suggested that bullying, monitoring, suspension, abandonment, and surveillance in schools and colleges, and at airports and borders, should be understood as belonging to a broader carceral ecology that produces Muslim boys as a threat: as terrorists-in-development or proto-terrorists. Recognizing this landscape helps nuance our understanding of how Muslim boys are pinned against matrices where overlapping yet distinct histories and practices of racialization are arrayed. For the fourteen-year-old clockmaker Ahmed, who is of Sudanese descent, threat is attached to both phenotype and religion, conjoining two longstanding discourses of difference: recall that my high school interlocutors immediately recognized gender, race, and religion as independent *and* overlapping factors in the school's overreaction to Ahmed's invention and their projection of what might happen to other (hypothetical) clockmakers. For Muslim boys categorized as white under U.S. federal census standards, like the five-year-old of Iranian descent whose airport detention Spicer tried to justify, fears related to national security—here, fear of Iran—can combine with other cultural markers, such as accents or food and clothing choices, to limit access to whiteness. The harassment of that young boy at the border reveals what Neda Maghbouleh describes as the volatility and fickleness of whiteness in relation to racially liminal groups.[75] But whiteness, as Patrick Casey has pointed out, can also shield white Muslims from prejudice—and Casey's conclusions about the countervailing impact of Muslim religious clothing dovetail with my high school students' intuitive sense that a girl who wore the hijab would be treated differently than a white Catholic schoolgirl.[76] When observing the Muslim experience in the United States, these

75. Neda Maghbouleh, *The Limits of Whiteness* (Stanford, Calif.: Stanford University Press, 2017).

76. Casey, "The Racialization of American Muslim Converts."

categories of difference (gender, race, religion) cannot be neatly sep-arated and are more helpfully understood as constellations whose relation to the center (Deleuze and Guattari's "White-Man face") shifts according to the context.

Nor can the complex experience of living as a Muslim boy in the United States be readily separated from the circumstances of perpetual war footing and the capitalist interests that fuel it. In an environment of constant fear—harnessed by beliefs that Muslim boys are proto-terrorists—militarization necessarily follows. This militarization is visible in the growth of the Countering Violent Extremism (CVE) workforce, expansion of the Transportation Security Administration (TSA), and the buildup of weapons for domestic peacekeeping purposes. Within three years of launch-ing its CVE initiative, the FBI had established CVE points of con-tact at twenty-six field offices, created a CVE coordinator at the Department of Homeland Security, and held trainings and resiliency exercises in seven cities.[77] During the Trump administration, ac-cording to a report by the Brennan Center for Justice, the amount of CVE funding going to law enforcement tripled, from $764,000 to $2,340,000.[78] The TSA was created just two months after 9/11 for the explicit purpose of preventing terrorist attacks. Its 2024 fiscal year budget request includes $11.2 billion, over sixty-one thousand positions, and over fifty-seven thousand full-time equivalents.[79] Whether profit is derived from supplying the Afghan war or from the expansion of the domestic security state, treating Muslim boy-

77. This information is summarized in a letter written by Texas Congressman Michael McCaul in his capacity as Chairman of the House Committee on Homeland Security. See Representative Michael McCaul letter, December 17, 2014, https://mccaul.house.gov/.

78. Faiza Patel, Andrew Lindsay, and Sophia DenUyl, "Countering Violent Extremism in the Trump Era," *Brennan Center for Justice*, June 15, 2018, https://www.brennancenter.org/our-work/research-reports/countering-violent-extremism-trump-era.

79. Department of Homeland Security, *TSA Budget Overview, Fiscal Year 2024* (Government of United States, 2023).

hood as a category of risk is profitable: the more thoroughly Muslim boys can be construed as proto-terrorists, the more money can be made by those who then get paid to watch, detect, and contain them. Without these antagonistic and frightening figures, the American empire might lose its coherence.

Returning to Rezwan's case, we can observe that the function of the proto-terrorist in the context of a capital-driven war footing also explains why instead of seeing Afghan refugees and white rural low-income people aligning against a war-profiteering elite (that sends low-income white people from rural Missouri to serve in the military and displaces Afghans or others whom they fight), we see antagonism between these groups. Some students at Rezwan's school made it very clear that he was not welcome; their perceptions of him were almost inevitably shaped by the same stereotypes and "threat" messaging that made Ahmed's teacher see a bomb when he brought a clock or made security guards at Dulles airport detain a five-year-old. Blame for war is displaced from state actors and capitalists onto ordinary people. Rezwan found himself on the wrong side of resentments that may be racialized in their expression, but that are arguably driven directly or indirectly by warfare capitalism. Such phobias around Muslims then impede cross-racial solidarity and substantial discussions around capitalist exploitation.[80]

80. Berlant and Warner make this observation about immigrants in Lauren Berlant and Michael Warner, *Sex in Public* (Durham, N.C.: Duke University Press, 1997), 549.

3. Instrumental Staging and Commercialization

AHMED MOHAMED'S 2015 ARREST was widely criticized as an example of racial profiling. The social media reaction was strong, with activists using hashtags like #IamAhmed and #IStandWithAhmed, to express support and condemn the mistreatment of the Muslim boy. Yet this backlash against the school's and police's overreach was quickly brought under control by state and capitalist elites, who rearticulated Ahmed as an "inventor" and a "budding scientist."[1] New York City Mayor Bill de Blasio issued a proclamation declaring September 28 "Ahmed Day" and coopted the incident to advance his "computer science for all" agenda.[2] He tweeted, "A young man builds a clock and starts a movement. Let's nurture tech creativ-

1. See, for example, Kate Briquelet, "Nerds Rage over Ahmed Mohamed's Clock," *The Daily Beast*, July 12, 2017, https://www .thedailybeast.com/nerds-rage-over-ahmed-mohameds-clock; Rachel Feltman, "#IStandWithAhmed: Scientists and the Public Surge to Support Boy Arrested for Homemade Clock," *The Washington Post*, September 16, 2015, https://www.washingtonpost.com/news/speaking-of-science/wp /2015/09/16/istandwithahmed-scientists-and-the-public-surge-to-support -boy-arrested-for-homemade-clock.
2. Kim Bellware, "Here's What Ahmed Mohamed Has Been Up to Since His Clock Arrest," *Huffington Post*, October 18, 2015, https:// www.huffingtonpost.com/entry/ahmed-mohamed-white-house_us _56239e6ae4b0bce34701009e.

ity w/ #CS4All, in NYC and everywhere."[3] New York City Public Advocate Letitia James let Ahmed sit in her chair in the council chambers,[4] Council Speaker Melissa Mark-Viverito took Ahmed and his family on a tour of City Hall, and Comptroller Scott Stringer gave him a framed commendation.[5] Stringer later tweeted, "All students should engage w/ science and technology—Ahmed Mohamed is a role model for all NYers #IStandWithAhmed."[6] President Obama even invited Ahmed to visit the White House.[7]

Technology firms also praised Ahmed's creativity: Microsoft sent him gifts; Facebook CEO Mark Zuckerberg invited him to visit the company. Ahmed received invitations from 3M and Google Science Fairs. These responses claimed innocence (lack of sin, malice, or wrongdoing) for Ahmed by reiterating the promise of youth and scientific innovation. On Facebook, Zuckerberg posted, "The future belongs to people like Ahmed," and U.S. Secretary of Education Arne Duncan said: "We need to be encouraging young engineers, not putting them in handcuffs."[8]

3. NYC Major (@NYCMayor), Twitter, September 28, 2015, 6:21 p.m., https://twitter.com/NYCMayor/status/648623610874187776.

4. See image here: Tish James, (@TishJames), "Thanks @ IStandWithAhmed for coming to visit NYC! Great showing you & fam around. Never stop dreaming & being you," Twitter, September 28, 2015, 4:14 p.m., https://twitter.com/TishJames/status/648591733194944512.

5. Yoav Gonen, "New York City Bigwigs Can't Get Enough of 'Terror' Clock Kid," NY Post, September 29, 2015, https://nypost.com/2015/09/29/new-york-city-bigwigs-cant-get-enough-of-terror-clock-kid/.

6. Office of New York City Comptroller, (@NYCComptroller), Twitter, September 28, 2015, 2:54 p.m., https://twitter.com/NYCComptroller/status/648571395853692928.

7. President Obama, (@POTUS44), "Cool clock, Ahmed. Want to bring it to the White House? We should inspire more kids like you to like science. It's what makes America great," September 16, 2015, 12:58 p.m., https://twitter.com/POTUS44/status/644193755814342656.

8. Mark Zuckerberg, "The future belongs to people like Ahmed," Facebook, September 15, 2015, https://www.facebook.com/zuck/posts/10102373304096361; Secretary Arne Duncan, "We need to be encouraging young engineers, not putting them in handcuffs. #IStandWithAhmed," Facebook, September 16, 2015, https://

This chapter examines the politics of such ostensibly positive portrayals of Muslim boys—portrayals that, at first glance, seem to counter the more dominant proto-terrorist framing. But as I will argue, such gestures of recognition work through abstraction and exceptionalism (one among many), leaving intact the originary construction of Muslim boyhood as a state of threat. Exceptionalism, as Jasbir Puar writes, "paradoxically signals distinction from (to be unlike, dissimilar) as well as excellence (imminence, superiority)."[9] Accordingly, Ahmed's portrayal does little to reframe the threat associated with Muslim boys as a collective. It does, however, enable state and capitalist elites to instrumentally stage the Muslim boy and present themselves as race-, gender-, and religion-neutral. I call this practice "commodity antiracism," where antiracism is commercialized and buys the elites goodwill. In a second case considered for this chapter, we see commercialization working differently: here, a young Muslim man who actually engages in an act of terrorism in Boston ends up on the cover of *Rolling Stone*. I view this as an example of how profit-seeking corporations may reward Muslim boys with celebrity status and a cover image in their effort to extract profit from those who desire to *see* terrorism.

In both of these cases, we can observe the instrumental staging of Muslim boys in the service of capital. These practices are extractive, in that they extract goodwill and revenue for the elites and do little to challenge the dominant ideas associated with Muslim boys. In fact, the backlash that such depictions invite—even entice, as we will see in the case of *Rolling Stone*—may ultimately coalesce support around the stereotypes. These isolated instances of recognition can thus more appropriately be seen as constitutive of, rather than incidental to, the construction of Muslim boyhood as a threat.

---

www.facebook.com/SecretaryArneDuncan/posts/pfbid029shMNb3e CRYDF8iZzBowfKAgCcuiR4ayCvLbx8nSUZ4Y5pruzmoFpmx HTNGdQC62l.

9. Jasbir Puar, *Terrorist Assemblages* (Durham, N.C.: Duke University Press, 2007): 3.

Commodity Antiracism

In the backlash that rapidly succeeded the initial accusations, Ahmed was allowed, by way of public recognition and proclamation, to reenter the domain of youthful potential and promise—a zone of permitted experimentation that is too often restricted to white boys (or, as we will see below, may be granted to some nonwhites only if they adhere to the scripts of "model minority"). But support for Ahmed did not come by way of a public reckoning with the racialized and Islamophobic discrimination he had experienced; that discrimination was occluded behind the national celebration of his scientific potential. He was made "like us" through reference to the most cherished of liberal values—rationality and entrepreneurial spirit—characteristics that the dominant U.S. culture rarely recognizes in "irrational" Muslims. Ahmed was renarrativized from "terrorist/bad immigrant" to "good immigrant/future-tech-worker/ model minority."

The benevolence afforded to Ahmed was instrumental and strategic: through symbolic gestures (invitations to visit or apply to a program), capitalist corporations and liberal politicians framed themselves as anti-racist and pro-Muslim, even as they sidestepped responsibility for creating structural changes to counter anti-Muslim racism. When they commended Ahmed's creativity and his interest in technology, representatives of firms like Facebook and political leaders like Obama were capitalizing on an opportunity to create goodwill for themselves. I view these gestures as a form of *commodity antiracism*. I fashion this term inspired by the formulation of commodity feminism by Goldman, Heath, and Smith.[10] As a practice, commodity antiracism appropriates the ideals of antiracism (in this case, those ideals also dovetail with pro-youth, pro-technology, and pro-Muslim logics), empties them of their political

10. Robert Goldman, Deborah Heath, and Sharon Smith, "Commodity Feminism," *Critical Studies in Mass Communication* 8, no. 3 (1991): 333–51.

significance, and then offers them back to the public as a commodity that builds goodwill for the likes of Mark Zuckerberg or Bill de Blasio. Offering this commodified antiracism to a public whose gratitude is assumed, the corporate or political leaders can display their antiracism—and do so without any meaningful commitment to practicing antiracism within their own organizations.

On the receiving end of this performative benevolence, when a Black Muslim boy like Ahmed gains entry to the domain of innocence, that access is tentative, contingent, and non-transferable. Unlike race, which in the case of Brown and Black people is naturalized, the capacity for scientific achievement is not—and on the occasions when it is racialized, it is coded as white or affixed to the model minority paradigm, which perpetuates anti-Blackness. The inclusive gestures toward Ahmed and his "innocence"—not just his guilt or innocence in relation to the bomb-making accusations, but in relation to the more abstract innocence of childhood—were hotly debated on right-wing media platforms, a contestation that recalls our earlier discussion of comparative innocence and criminality. Fox News host Anna Kooiman insisted that Ahmed was "not as innocent as he seems."[11] She cited a minor incident, "[B]lowing soap bubbles in a bathroom," for which Ahmed was suspended, as evidence of his school disciplinary problems.[12] That incident itself reminds us that a seemingly innocuous action can be read as offensive—even deserving of suspension—when it is performed by a Black Muslim boy. The threat-innocence binary was ruthlessly exposed when Ahmed's teacher said he was "one of those kids that could either be CEO of a company or head of a gang."[13] It is worth

11. As cited in Dominique Mosbergen, "Fox News Host: Teen Clockmaker Is 'Not as Innocent as He Seems,'" *The Huffington Post*, October 6, 2015, https://www.huffpost.com/entry/fox-host-teen-clockmaker-ahmed -mohamed_n_560e4826e4b0dd85030b8ae4.

12. Mosbergen.

13. Mosbergen.

noting here that both Ahmed's adherents and his detractors appear equally comfortable in holding innocence as a gift they can choose to bestow or withhold.

Other efforts to recast Ahmed as a threat more explicitly invoked the proto-terrorist trope. Robert Spencer, director of a popular far-right blog called *Jihad Watch,* pondered the "ominous implications" of Ahmed Day for New York's residents and stoked fear by pushing Ahmed's factually harmless device back toward the bomb that anti-Muslim prejudice preferred to imagine: "Will some enterprising young jihadi take advantage of this favorable new situation, and make a clock that really is a bomb? If that ever happens, will Mayor de Blasio apologize for Ahmed Day? Will Barack Obama apologize for feting the lad at the White House? Of course not."[14] Comments on Spencer's article invoked language that distanced Ahmed from innocence—insisting that the fourteen-year-old had full knowledge and agency—together with some "terrorism" messaging. Commenting under the name Steve Bryant, one reader focused particularly on knowledge and intent: "The obvious nature and intent of the little asshole is so much so that Mad Magazine could have run it as a satirical lead feature.... The boy *knew exactly what he was doing* (or his handlers did) and they have been successful beyond their wildest dreams" (emphasis added). Another commentator (screen name: jtrollla) called him "Islamobrat" and yet another (screen name: Lilith Wept) proposed a solution: "Hopefully we can just do something like declare that Islam is not a religion, but a socio political system that has as a goal the over thoro [*sic*] of all non islamic goverments [*sic*], that Islam is not compatable [*sic*] with, can simply not co exist with American laws and way of life." This comment is illuminating in the parallel it draws between the

14. Robert Spencer, "Ahmed Day and the End of 'If You See Something, Say Something,'" *FrontPage Magazine*, October 1, 2015, https://www.frontpagemag.com/fpm/260303/ahmed-day-and-end-if-you-see-something-say-robert-spencer.

Muslim child's innocence and his religion: as the child is presumed to exist outside the pale of innocence, so is Islam readily expelled from the realm of religions of God.

Ahmed and his family decided to move to Qatar a month after the incident to avoid ongoing harassment. In 2017, a federal judge dismissed their lawsuit against the Irving Independent School District due to lack of evidence. U.S. District Judge Sam Lindsay of the Northern District of Texas noted in the ruling that the plaintiff (Ahmed's father) did not offer any facts to demonstrate that the school district employees had treated Ahmed "differently than other similarly situated students, and that the unequal treatment was based on religion or race."[15] Although the judge allowed the Mohameds to submit additional facts to amend claims that were deemed "factually deficient," the refiled case was also dismissed in 2018.

Commercialization of Terrorism

In April 2013, twenty-year-old Dzhokhar Tsarnaev, together with his older brother, planted pressure cooker bombs near the finish line of the Boston Marathon, killing three people and injuring hundreds. Unlike Ahmed, Dzhokhar was, in fact, a bomber.[16] *Rolling Stone* ran a cover story on Dzhokhar in August 2013, just another entry in the magazine's coverage of popular culture, music, and politics (Figure 2). The cover line—"How a Popular, Promising Student Was Failed by His Family, Fell Into Radical Islam, and Became a Monster"—carried the now-familiar elements of a dysfunctional family, Islam as an aberration, and Muslims as monstrous. Despite the established storyline—consistent with how Muslim young men and boys are generally presented in Western media—*Rolling Stone* was widely criticized for the cover. The Mayor of Boston said it

15. BBC News, "'Clock Boy' Discrimination Case Thrown Out by Texas Judge," *BBC News*, May 19, 2017.
16. Dzhokhar Tsarnaev was sentenced to death; however, the Department of Justice has put a moratorium on federal executions.

"reward[ed] a terrorist with celebrity treatment"; others saw it as "insulting" and "glamorizing the face of terror."[17] Magazine-cover commodification of terrorism is not uncommon and it is rarely so controversial. Osama bin Laden has repeatedly been featured on the covers of *TIME* and *Newsweek;* Omar Mateen, Adolf Hitler, Timothy McVeigh, Ted Kaczynski, Jeffrey Dahmer, and Charles Manson have also appeared on magazine covers.[18] Why then the pushback on a story that labeled its subject a monster?

The problem in Dzhokhar's case was the photo. *Rolling Stone's* words call him a monster, but what we see on that cover is a tousle-haired white youth; with his carefully styled facial hair and T-shirt, he could easily be a young rock star. Indeed, some readers compared the image to Justin Bieber's 2011 "Super Boy" *Rolling Stone* cover (Figure 3), and others to an iconic cover photo of 1960s rock star Jim Morrison (Figure 4).[19] *Rolling Stone* came under attack because it disturbed the prevailing "culture of the visual" associated with terrorists and terrorism. Hal Foster theorizes such visual culture in a way that links the physiological mechanism of seeing with socialization.[20] The cover photo successfully evaded the racialized frames that readers had long associated with terrorism. It flipped the expectation of Brown assailant and white victim that the *wSieci* Polish magazine cover catered to; instead, it centered the face and

17. Office of the Mayor City of Boston, *Thomas M. Menino, Statement,* June 17, 2013, https://twitter.com/ABC/status/357584909994455040; Julie Cannold, Mayra Cuevas, and Joe Sterling, "Rolling Stone Cover of Bombing Suspect Called 'Slap' to Boston," *CNN,* July 18, 2013, https://www.cnn.com /2013/07/17/studentnews/tsarnaev-rolling-stone-cover/index.html.

18. See October 1, 2001, November 26, 2001, November 25, 2002, and May 20, 2011 covers of *TIME;* November 16, 2011 cover of *Newsweek.*

19. See these comparisons: Anonymous, "'Callous and Crass: Some Thoughts on Rolling Stone's Cover," *Wbur,* July 17, 2013, https://www.wbur .org/news/2013/07/17/tsarnaev-rolling-stone-cover; David McCormack, "Outrage over 'Sick' Rolling Stone Cover," *Daily Mail,* July 16, 2013, https:// www.dailymail.co.uk/news/article-2366501/Tsarnaev-Rolling-Stone-cover -causes-outrage-glamorizing-glorifying-Boston-bomber.html.

20. Hal Foster, *Vision and Visuality* (Seattle: Bay Press, 1988): ix.

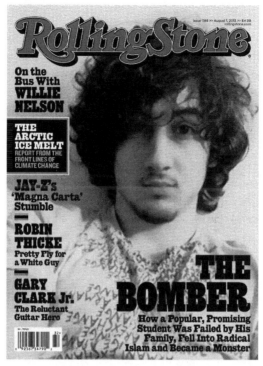

Figure 2. *Rolling Stone* cover featuring Dzhokhar Tsarnaev.

torso of a young, white man whom the magazine invites readers to see as both victim (of radicalization) and perpetrator (of terrorism). Looking at a cover image of an attractive could-be-rock-star youth, readers were robbed of meanings they had already begun to create about Muslims, and Black and Brown boys, including, perhaps, a belief that subjecting Brown-presenting Muslims to rigorous surveillance is all that is needed to identify the "leakage" that is supposed to be both inevitable and visible. Readers were angry because they couldn't make sense of a cover that belied their certainties, in this case, their certainty in associating terrorism with Muslims, and Muslims with Brownness and menace. As *Washington Post* media critic Erik Wemple points out, Dzhokhar defied assumptions that terrorists are animalistic: The photo "humanize[d]" him for people who otherwise "want[ed] to see him as an animal from Day One."[21] Wemple goes on to connect the photo to a narrative in which Dzhokhar exists as "our" friend: "The facts are he wasn't an animal, at least to his peer group, for the longest time. They remember him as a dear friend. That's a problem, because he was part of our society and he turned on it by all indications, or allegedly."

Rolling Stone had committed two cultural "sins." First is a sin of omission—*Rolling Stone* should have made him look Brown and threatening, which would have reinforced readers' prior understanding of Muslim boys. And second is a sin of commission—*Rolling Stone* made him look white and attractive, engaging the reader's positive emotional or aesthetic response, thus deliberately provoking the reader's anger at what seems to them like a bait and switch. The cover image entices the viewer to respond emotionally to Dzhokhar as a sympathetic, attractive figure even as the text pulls against identification and sympathy. It makes a connection between whiteness and terrorism that Americans have long resisted in the face of growing evidence. Caroline Corbin has argued that the American public persistently reserves the label of terrorist for Brown Muslims and resists using this label for white people who commit acts of violence.[22] Even in recent years as far-right violence has been increasing and as the FBI has developed new naming regimes for domestic crimes, it has steered clear from labeling white violence "terrorism." Corbin's work indicates that this reluctance derives not from a narrow law-enforcement bias but from a larger crisis of racial myths that include assumptions about white innocence and white superiority. The FBI's 2019 "Confronting White Supremacy" statement before the House Oversight and Reform Committee, for instance, uses such terms

21. As cited in Cannold, Cuevas, and Sterling, "Rolling Stone."
22. Caroline Corbin, "Terrorists Are Always Muslim but Never White," *Fordham Law Review* 86, no. 2 (2017): 455–86.

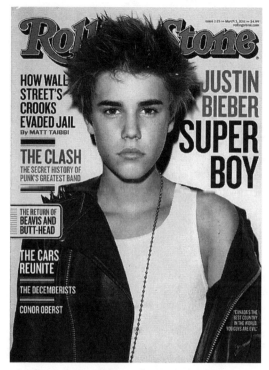

Figure 3. *Rolling Stone* March 2011 cover featuring Justin Bieber.

as "domestic violence," "lone offenders," "homegrown violence," or "hate crimes," but does not categorize particular trends or offenses as white—even when white individuals are the overwhelming majority of perpetrators in a given category. In a remarkable contrast, the FBI used the phrase "Black Identity Extremists" in a 2017 intelligence assessment to justify surveillance of Black people, including Black activists.[23] In 2019, after legislators expressed

23. FBI, *Black Identity Extremists Likely Motivated to Target Law Enforcement Officers* (FBI Counterterrorism Division, 2017).

Figure 4. *Rolling Stone* April 1991 cover featuring Jim Morrison.

concern over the phrase and its implications, the FBI introduced a new phrase: "Racially Motivated Violent Extremism."[24] Today the phrase "Racially and Ethnically Motivated Violent Extremism" is used. These new phrases effectively group white supremacists with Black activists, placing Black people and organizations protesting police brutality in the same category as those who insist on the superiority of the white race.

24. Byron Tau, "FBI Abandons Use of Term 'Black Identity Extremism,'" *The Wall Street Journal*, July 23, 2019, https://www.wsj.com /articles/fbi-abandons-use-of-terms-black-identity-extremism-11563921355.

It is against this broader cultural resistance to view white-coded individuals as terrorists that some *Rolling Stone* readers set out to search for images of Dzhokhar that *Rolling Stone* could—or "should"—have used instead to convey the "truth." They tried to move Dzhokhar out of whiteness—or situate him within the familiar Brown and Black visual economy where, in their minds, he belonged. Consider an article on the website of Boston's *NPR* news station, *WBUR*. Its author suggests why an alternate black-and-white image of Dzhokhar would have been more appropriate:

> It's a black-and-white photo in which Tsarnaev, with puffy and narrowed eyes, looks into the camera. He does not look friendly or cute. He looks—or is trying to look—menacing but doesn't quite pull it off. To me, having read the Rolling Stone story, it looks like a photo of someone in the middle of a transition from "popular, promising student" to "monster." And a black-and-white photo on the cover of the usually colorful Rolling Stone would have really made a visual statement.[25]

In the game of racializing, people may be instrumentally staged—whitened or darkened—in the service of a larger ideological project. *Rolling Stone* wanted to play on Dzhokhar's white-passing to suggest that someone who is "one of us" could be turned (hinting at the "at risk" narrative), while the readers who pushed back against the cover image wanted to force him into the category of "a risk."[26] They accordingly proposed photos that darkened him to conform with their expectations that a Muslim immigrant should be nonwhite in appearance. From that visual confirmation of racialized Muslimness, the slide into proto-terrorism is easy and predictable.

Instead of trying to better understand the complexity around political violence, media figures who commented on this controversial portrayal of Dzhokhar chose to stay within older frames of

25. Anonymous, "Callous and Crass."
26. See also a discussion of how the Tsarnaev brothers were stripped of whiteness in Nazli Kibria, Tobias Watson, and Saher Selod, "Imagining the Radicalized Muslim," *Sociology of Race and Ethnicity* 4, no. 2 (2018): 192–205.

fear and xenophobia. CNN journalist S. E. Cupp worried explicitly about innocence: "To me, seems @RollingStone isn't glamorizing terrorism, but proving that it can look innocent and young and attractive. Important lesson . . . I hope every young @RollingStone reader [who] reads Tsarnaev story, realizes that radical Islam's here, can even infect a young Jim Morrison."[27] The term "infect" here harkens back to our earlier discussion about purity/impurity; here, the health of a nation is undermined by "radical Islam" (viewed as a disease or pollutant in this case). When Cupp mentions 1960s white rock star Jim Morrison, she reminds her audience of the whiteness that radicalized Muslims now purportedly threaten. Tommy Vietor, former White House national security spokesman, expressed similar concerns: "a disaffected U.S. kid could see this and think terrorists are afforded rock star status."[28]

But the presence of Dzhokhar—a boy of Chechnyan decent from Kyrgyzstan—in Cambridge also recalls the complexity of Rezwan's status as a refugee from a U.S.-driven war in Afghanistan. Dzhokhar's family had applied for political asylum in the United States following actions by Russia (annexation and ethnic cleansing) in Chechnya and Kyrgyzstan. But after arriving in America, he reportedly became particularly concerned about U.S. imperial wars against Muslims. Might we read Dzhokhar as responding to a broader pattern in which the United States engages in colonizing violence against Muslims, even though his relationship to that experience is indirect?

Rolling Stone managing editor Will Dana defended the cover as an apt image, belonging to a story about "what an incredibly normal

27. S. E. Cupp, (@secupp), Twitter, July 17, 2013, 10:48 p.m., https:// twitter.com/secupp/status/357693445332140035; and, S. E. Cupp, (@ secupp), Twitter, July 17, 2013, 10:53 p.m., https://twitter.com/secupp/status /357694566343770112.

28. As cited in Dylan Byers, "There's Nothing Wrong with Rolling Stone's Tsarnaev Cover," *Politico*, July 17, 2013, https://www.politico.com /blogs/media/2013/07/theres-nothing-wrong-with-rolling-stones-tsarnaev -cover-168607.

kid [Dzhokhar] seemed like to those who knew him best back in Cambridge [Mass.]"[29] But beyond this storyline we might also ask how our aesthetic demands to "see the other" (in this case, terrorists) can influence supply. Dzhokhar's image is disturbing in the sense that it is meant to titillate and excite but also to extract the viewer's energy through the dissonance experienced. And *Rolling Stone* is more comfortable than are many of its readers, with a disruptive image of Dzhokhar on the cover, because the magazine stands to profit from its readers' discomfort. There is an indisputably economic dimension to this visual exchange. *Rolling Stone* responds to a public demand to see terrorism, and it makes money whether or not it shows them the picture of terrorism they expect. In fact, the magazine potentially makes more money by showing readers an image that counters their expectations. While a few retailers such as Star Market, CVS, and Tedeschi Food Shops decided not to carry the *Rolling Stone* issue, sales for the issue were twice the magazine's average.[30] *AdWeek* ranked the Dzhokhar Tsarnaev cover as the "Hottest Cover of the Year."[31] It may therefore be more helpful to read this cover image (together with more conventional photos of known or accused terrorists) as responding to a public demand to see violence in an economy that philosopher Sayak Valencia has termed as "gore capitalism."[32] Rather than pushing us toward

29. Eyder Prealta, "Rolling Stone's Tsarnaev Cover: What's Stirring Such Passion?" *NPR All Things Considered*, July 17, 2013, https://www.npr .org/sections/thetwo-way/2013/07/17/202956379/rolling-stones-tsarnaev -cover-whats-stirring-such-passion.

30. Ricardo Lopez, "Rolling Stone Sales Doubled for Issue Featuring Boston Bomber," *Los Angeles Times*, August 1, 2013, https://www.latimes .com/business/la-fi-mo-rolling-stone-sales-boston-bomber-20130801-story .html.

31. Steve Annear, "The Dzhokhar Tsarnaev 'Rolling Stone' Cover Won Adweek's 'Hottest Cover of the Year,'" *Boston Magazine*, December 4, 2013, https://www.bostonmagazine.com/news/2013/12/04/adweek-hot-list-2013 -dzhokhar-tsarnaev/.

32. Sayak Valencia, *Gore Capitalism* (Cambridge, Mass.: MIT Press, 2018).

moralistic arguments for or against *Rolling Stone,* thinking with Valencia directs us toward questions about the commodification of terrorism across a range of contexts—magazine covers, but also books, social media, and television—and how consumer demand to see terror/terrorists shapes this exchange.

The Cunning of Capitalist Benevolence

Why is it that the moments and images discussed in this chapter are not felt more directly as counterexamples prompting logical reevaluation of the "knowledge" so painfully constructed at the expense of Muslim boys? The answer may lie in the fact that these are cases of instrumental staging in the service of capital, and not much more.

When Ahmed is celebrated, it is his inventiveness and scientific acumen that are celebrated and not the individual who possesses these attributes. The possession of these traits—not typically associated with Muslim boys as socially constructed in America— allows Ahmed to step outside the enclosed space assigned to Muslim boyhood and briefly access innocence. Ahmed's access is incidental; it is not shared with the community of other Muslim boys and hence does not destabilize the dominant constructions of Muslim boyhood. Capitalist benevolence operates through abstraction or exception. Elsewhere I have discussed how such abstractions work in relation to Muslim girls. Analyzing the case of Malala Yousafzai, I have argued that exceptionalizing Malala is a strategy to isolate her and thus sustain the trope of victimized Muslim women.[33] In this way, her courage (as a Muslim woman), her pursuit of education, and even her critique of U.S. imperialism are radically disassociated from the category of Muslim women, keeping the latter as politically useful victimized subjects of Muslim men and Islam. In both

33. Shenila Khoja-Moolji, "Reading Malala: (De)(Re)Territorialization of Muslim Collectivities," *Comparative Studies of South Asia, Africa, and the Middle East* 35, no. 3 (2015): 539–56.

instances, the instrumental staging after the effect enables politicians and corporations to buy the public's goodwill and mitigate any simmering backlash.

The instrumental staging in the case of Dzhokhar is more obvious: his rock-star likeness and white-passing elicit backlash that *Rolling Stone* then proceeds to monetize. There is no real effort to humanize him, to use the dissonance created to destabilize preconceived notions about Islam and Muslims. Instead, the staging reiterates stereotypes of how the nation is at risk of being breached by Islamic "monsters"—foreign, and now domestic as well. Commodity antiracism and commercial terrorism then work in similar ways: Mayor de Blasio gains support for his computer science program and *Rolling Stone* nearly doubles its sales for the issue. Meanwhile, little is done to reframe Muslim boys in the eyes of those who consume these instrumental stagings.

4. Whiteness, Hindutva, and Impurity

IN AMERICA, Muslims are at once hypervisible—in the sense that they are the focus of significant interest—and invisible—because they are afforded a limited set of subject positions through which to recognize themselves. And while, since 9/11, scholars have paid increasing attention to representations of Muslims, studies of the gendered dimensions of this representation (including my own work) have tended to focus on the binary of the so-called "violent" Muslim man and "disempowered" Muslim woman. In this book I have tried to introduce nuance to this discussion by recognizing Muslim boyhood as a distinct political form that conjoins past actual terror with future anticipated terror. In this ideological project, Muslim boys get constructed as proto-terrorists. This construction is both produced by, and authorizes, statist practices of preemptive enclosure: surveillance and punishment. And while we can see this through the lens of racialization—imbuing Muslim boys with impurity or threat—capitalism is at work here, too. If and where a proto-terrorist exists, the state (and its proxies) must maintain a war footing; businesses might even stage terrorism in cultural forms (such as magazines) to meet consumer demand to see past and present terror. Racial and capitalist logics then go hand in hand.

Throughout the book therefore I have examined how statist and capitalist forces shape Muslim boyhood in American public culture.

In this chapter, I highlight how these forces unfold at the scalar level of interiority, influencing the ordinary, intimate lives of boys. What does it feel like to walk down a city street or ride the subway as a Muslim boy when public culture is so thoroughly saturated by the message that you are a proto-terrorist? This is not to posit the discursive form as deterministic, but in the mode of Allen Feldman, to ask how political forms as historical narrative configurations mediate experience and are also actively transformed when social actors inhabit them.[1] I include some further findings from focus groups with Muslim boys in Queens, New York—whose opinions we have already heard regarding how race, gender, and perceived religious affiliation can shape school authorities' disciplinary responses. When we consider how these boys navigate public spaces, we see in practice what racialization feels like. And insofar as racialization demarcates a pure, innocent, non-raced center, we can also understand my interlocutors' experiences as the very means through which whiteness manifests in this world.

Invoking Muslim boyhood as a heuristic device, I close with a brief discussion on its appearance in a different context: India in the grips of a rising ethnonationalist movement, Hindutva. Muslim boyhood here is constructed as a threat to the ethno-religious purity of the Hindu *rashtra* (nation). Instead of an exhaustive comparison, the brief discussion about India hints at promising opportunities for further investigation and analysis. If we think outward from Deleuze and Guattari's framing of race as a constellation of impurities conferred by a system of domination, we can see how Muslim boyhood, as a state of impurity, is mobilized to invent different states of purity: whiteness in the United States, and religious and ethnic absolutism in India. Tracing Muslim boyhood across global contexts can thus reveal local specificities while also showing how these iterations are nonetheless connected in their operation as a foil against which innocence and purity are defined.

1. Allen Feldman, *Formations of Violence* (Chicago: University of Chicago Press, 1991): 15.

Feeling Racialization

For decades now, nonprofit organizations and policy makers have focused their attention on afterschool programs to target "under-served" or "at-risk" youth.[2] The stated purposes of such programs are to prevent delinquency and encourage responsible citizenship so that youth can succeed in the neoliberal state. I met my interlocutors through one such program—Young Men's Leadership Program—aimed at South Asian youth. While the program takes place at multiple sites, since my interest was in meeting with Muslim youth, the staff directed me to those schools where participants were predom-inantly Muslim. The five focus groups I conducted in New York in 2017 engaged twenty-six nonwhite boys. The immediate goal of this inquiry was to gauge participants' reactions to the arrest of the five-year-old boy at Dulles airport earlier that year and Ahmed Mohamed's arrest—an event that had taken place a couple of years earlier and received considerable media attention. I also had a more general interest in examining the kinds of conversations that the discussion of these events might prompt. Focus group conversations were therefore open-ended.

The experience of Muslim boys as they move through New York City cannot, of course, be disentangled from their experience as racially coded subjects. We can thus see their experience as the very matter of whiteness's becoming—how it truncates wellbeing, how it compels bodies to move in certain ways (or even shrink), and how it impinges on imagination. In formulating my analysis in this way, I echo Sara Ahmed, who reminds us that whiteness is not an "ontological given."[3] It can be best described, instead, as "an ongoing and unfinished history, which orientates bodies

2. Robert Halpern, "A Different Kind of Child Development Institution: The History of After-School Programs for Low-Income Children," *Teachers College Record* 104, no. 2 (2002): 178–211.

3. Sara Ahmed, "A Phenomenology of Whiteness," *Feminist Theory* 8, no. 2 (2007): 150.

in specific directions, affecting how they 'take up' space."[4] The racialization of Muslim boys that I have been describing in this book is how whiteness (that which is pure or not-raced) (re)makes the world and limits nonwhite Muslim bodies to specific, often enclosed spaces and constrained behaviors. It is these feelings and behaviors—how Muslim boys "take up space" or not—that are the focus of this section.

But whiteness is not experienced uniformly by everyone. As we will see below, a Black or Brown Muslim boy might face certain social pressures of whiteness that he shares with other nonwhite boys, but his experience of these pressures is undoubtedly layered by the public cultural expressions that posit Muslim boys as risk. Even when a boy does not don specifically Muslim markers of identity, he might still carry with him memories (personal and collective) of differential treatment that would not be visible to the people who sit next to him on the bus or the police who stop him on the street but would shape how he internalizes and responds to their looks, comments, or commands. We thus encounter various constellations of individual experiences of racialization which are nonetheless interpreted within a shared Muslim minoritarian sense.

"It Is Unfair"

My focus group participants found Ahmed's arrest absurd: "the school overreacted"; "the reaction to the whole thing was overboard." One focus group laughed at the clear mismatch between action and reaction:

> **PARTICIPANT A:** How did they find it [Ahmed's clock]?
> **MODERATOR:** He was just taking it out of his bag.
> **PARTICIPANT B:** And they just thought, that's a bomb?

The group breaks out in laughter.

---

4. Ahmed, 150.

PARTICIPANT C: If it's your [school] project, how would you avoid that? Like what am I supposed to do? Not hand it in?

The group breaks out in laughter again.

A participant in another focus group made a similar point: "That's an example of overachieving gone wrong [laughter]." To which a fellow student added, in an exasperated tone, "So he got in trouble for doing his project?" Participants continued: "How do you mistake that for a bomb?" and "It is unfair that they took him away."

Absurd and unfair though Ahmed's treatment may have been, my participants did not view his experience as an aberration. Some thought a similar incident would be unlikely at their own predominantly-Brown schools, but in a white school setting, they could easily imagine being arrested just as Ahmed was. There is good reason for this. Juvenile court systems have long targeted Black and Latinx boys; although many of my interlocutors were of South Asian descent, they now face a carceral system that uses on them techniques honed through decades of policing Black life. Writing in 2002, Gary Smith observed a distinct shift in the juvenile system away from the courts' original project of rehabilitation and toward punishment.[5] Many states made it easier for minors to be prosecuted as adults, relaxed confidentiality policies, increased penalties, and in some cases, lowered the minimum age for execution. California Proposition 21, the Gang Violence and Juvenile Crime Prevention Act, which passed in 2000, allowed a youth as young as fourteen years old to be tried as an adult. When that proposition was being discussed, proponents represented youth of color, and Black youth specifically, as "super-predators." Some of those trends, such as the age when minors can be executed, have reversed in more recent years. The Supreme Court banned execution of those under age eighteen in 2005 and there is ongoing effort to raise that age

5. Gary Smith, "Remorseless Young Predators: The Bottom Line of 'Caging Children," in *Growing Up Postmodern,* ed. Ronald Strickland (Blue Ridge Summit, Pa.: Rowman and Littlefield, 2002), 66–67.

to include young adults. While the country has pulled back from some extremes, it has still not necessarily moved toward rehabilitation. Debates around how much penalty is appropriate abound and many of the harsh punishments enacted twenty years ago are still on the books.

Furthermore, the twenty-first century has seen a significant increase in surveillance—the use of security cameras, presence of police in schools, and Stop-and-Frisk program[6]—which means a higher likelihood that Black and Brown boys face arrest. The plea-bargain system is another factor in the ongoing over-punishment of Black and Brown youth: because many of the harsh sentencing guidelines of the late twentieth century are still applicable, the accused who cannot afford a private attorney are likely to be guided by their pro bono attorney to take a plea rather than risk the harsh sentencing that could result from a jury trial. Black and Brown boys thus continue to be disproportionately affected by the carceral state. Against this background, my focus group participants explained the practices and maneuvers they had developed, both in and out of school, to avoid experiences like Ahmed's.

Self-Surveillance

Several participants emphasized visible changes of clothing style or behavior: "Whenever I am getting on a bus, and of course I have my hoodie on, I always make sure to take my hoodie off right in front of everyone in the bus so like no one has any ideas or anything." Another added: "I have changed my style. I don't wear hoodies anymore." When they walk at night and a white girl is ahead of

---

6. In 2013, a U.S. district court ruled that NYPD's Stop-and-Frisk program violated the U.S. Constitution. Racial disparities have however persisted. In 2022, according to New York Civil Liberties Union, 93 percent of those who were stopped were nonwhite and 65 percent were not given a summons or arrested (New York Civil Liberties Union, "Stop-and-Frisk Data," https://www.nyclu.org/en/stop-and-frisk-data, accessed August 23, 2023).

them, they "slow down," "take a different route," and "have my hands exposed" because they know of occasions when girls have felt uncomfortable and called the police. These teenage boys have noticed people "move their bags when they see me pass by."

At other times, rather than consciously performing harmlessness, they try to make themselves invisible: "I don't stand out. I try to be mellow. I don't do things extra," and "I just mind my business, don't do anything suspicious. Don't look at anybody." While my participants strive to avoid police officers and security personnel and "don't talk back to cops," they may still find themselves in difficult situations with them. One participant, Rahim, explained encounters with police in his neighborhood:

> Whenever I am walking on the Ave and have my headphones in, they stare me down. So it's like I always make sure I have to take off my headphones and make sure I am not doing anything. And it gets annoying from time to time because they do random searches but they only do it to people who aren't white, which I tend to see a lot. Like one time the police officer was so rude, he took all my stuff and he threw it on the floor. He was looking through my bag and like okay so I am gonna have to put all this back in, for nothing, cuz you aren't gonna find anything.

Frantz Fanon said, "In the white world the man of color encounters difficulties in the development of his bodily schema," for that development is structured by "the 'historic-racial' schema."[7] The gaze of the police officer, his careless handling of Rahim's bag and its contents, belong to that "historic-racial" schema, which ultimately racializes Rahim—and here I am alluding to Deleuze and Guattari's definition of race as a practice of domination.

While Rahim's experience is one that he shares with other nonwhite boys—being stopped by police and having belongings dumped out on the street is not exclusively experienced by those who are Muslim—a Muslim boy may live that reality differently

7. Fanon, *Black Skin, White Masks*, 110–11.

because it is layered with experiences that are specific to his religion. Said differently, he may experience these events and related feelings as part of a Muslim commons, a shared Muslim minoritarian sense. Thus my participants also talked of encounters where they felt that it was their (or their relatives') religious identity that stood out to the agents or police. One participant from Bangladesh recounted his father's harassment at the airport: "When you are at the airport, you want to be especially cautious . . . if you have a beard, you better cut it. . . . Oh my . . . My dad had a long beard, he cut it and they were like 'yo, you have to come over here' and we spent like two hours in that thing." Some Muslims wear a beard to emulate Prophet Muhammad. In popular culture it is associated with religious conservatism and prejudicially linked with extremism. Isolating religion from race, as I noted in chapter 1, is not a priority in my work. Following Mawani and Patel, I see Islam as being thoroughly integrated into assumptions about racial alterity in North America. It is less important for me to identify whether Rahim is mistreated because he is a Muslim or because he is an immigrant or coded as Brown. Muslimness, migrant status, and phenotype all work together as a connective regime in the eyes of the police officer who emptied Rahim's bag onto the sidewalk. In such circumstances the body reacts by making itself small, by eradicating its uniqueness: "Do what everybody else is doing"; "wear the same clothes"; "act the same way"; "select hamburger over chicken *karahi*" and "work on English language accents."

Managing Affect

Affect is central in the practices of self-surveillance described above. My participants managed their affect by trying to be "friendly" to everyone: "I try to be very friendly to people so they don't start getting nasty ideas" and "I smile a lot and offer to pick up bags for old white women at baggage claim." They described how they intentionally spoke softly and worked to appear "mellow" in white-dominated public settings, taking personal responsibility for calming the nerves of those around them—people who have been educated to read them in terms of threat.[8] They tried to "smile more" and appear "jolly." That my participants managed their affect in public is not surprising. They are deeply aware that they are being watched, not only by security officials but also by fellow passengers in an airport, travelers on a bus, or riders on a subway. Their fears are not unwarranted: the Transportation Security Administration's Behavior Detection and Analysis Program (previously called Screening Passengers by Observation Techniques) trains officers dressed in casual clothes to identify passengers exhibiting signs of suspicious behaviors (stress, fear, deception). TSA's own employees from Boston have criticized this program as specifically targeting people from racially marginalized groups.[9]

My participants' practices of intentional softening and calming are also informed by a long history in which Muslim men have been associated with an excess of emotion, particularly rage. We see that association on *Newsweek* magazine's cover page from September 28, 2012. Under the title "Muslim Rage," a group of Brown men, mouths wide open, protest—presumably angrily, presumably at an anti-U.S. rally, and presumably in some part of the Muslim world. That is a long list of presumptions, but *Newsweek* seems to have realized that most readers would make them. A decade earlier, on September 28, 2001, *Newsweek* had featured a similar cover image where a young Muslim boy held a gun, under the header "Why do they hate us? The roots of Islamic rage—and what we can do about it." In this construction, "they" are taken to task for unfairly directing rage at a majoritarian "us." Again, the expectation of excess affect is not exclusively reserved for Muslim men. In "Feeling Brown," José

8. Adult Muslims also engage in such forms of self-surveillance (see Nadine Naber, "The Rules of Forced Engagement: Race, Gender, and the Culture of Fear Among Arab Immigrants in San Francisco Post-9/11," *Cultural Dynamics* 18, no. 3 [2006]: 235–67).

9. Kelly Dickerson, "Yes, the TSA Is Probably Profiling You," *The Intercept*, May 6, 2015.

Muñoz argues that "standard models of United States citizenship are based on a national affect . . . This 'official' national affect, a mode of being in the world primarily associated with white middle-class subjectivity, reads most ethnic affect as inappropriate."[10] But affect may be projected differently onto different ethnic groups. Whereas in the case of Latinx people, it is the loud expression of joy that is viewed as unbecoming, in the case of Brown Muslim men, it is the public expression of discontent (or rage) that is the inappropriate affect. Rage is opposite to the emotional restraint demanded of middle-class subjects and assumed to characterize "us," the citizen-readers. When the magazines invoke rage, they are mobilizing a long history of characterizations of Arab men and Muslim men in colonizing discourses.[11] Muslims, young and old, perceive that they must modulate their reactions to fit the emotional space afforded by prescribed national affect (and we could extend this to national sartorial boundaries that exclude hoodies, beards, and hijab) or risk being marked as noncitizens.

Muslim boys are thus hypervigilant in spaces defined by whiteness or demarcated as white: "If you know where you are, you know what could happen. If you do certain things, you should alarm people of what you are doing. [Speaking of Ahmed] I would have went [sic] to my principal or even my science teacher and say that I am working on a project, an alarm clock, could you at least let the people in my area know." Commenting specifically on Ahmed's clock design, one participant said he would have thought

10. José Esteban Muñoz, "Feeling Brown," *Theatre Journal* 52, no. 1 (2000): 69.

11. See Julia Stephens, "The Politics of Muslim Rage: Secular Law and Religious Sentiment in Late Colonial India," *History Workshop Journal* 77, no. 1 (2014): 45–64. Popular media like Armstrong's newspaper article "The Brutal World of Sheep Fighting," assume violence/rage as the default state for Algerian/Muslim men and justify sheep fighting as a necessary outlet (Hannah Armstrong in *The Guardian*, February 16, 2018, https://www .theguardian.com/news/2018/feb/16/algeria-sheep-fighting-illegal-sport -angry-young-men).

more about the clock's appearance, would "not make it look like science-looking" and would have avoided "wires poking out."

But my participants also experience these acts of self-vigilance as burdensome. Bilal objected to the expectation that he should have to adapt his life and tastes:

> We shouldn't have to adapt but it's what we have to do now. In my neighborhood, there are four people taken by immigrant police, ICE. I think I heard that they were just knocking on doors and that's how they found people . . . We shouldn't have to adapt . . . We have people like Trump, basically higher ups in our system that set up standards and rules, how we should act, what we should say.

Faisal added:

> In African American households, when you get to a certain age, your parents, well, at least in my experience in [a] Muslim [household], you always get 'the talk' about how if you are ever suspected by any type of cop or any type of law enforcement you should like comply no matter what. Agree, no matter what. Don't talk out of line cuz they are afraid what can happen to . . . cuz you've seen videos of people like, police brutality everywhere. And it's like, like, I got this same talk at age six and that's a pretty young age to be worrying about that kind of thing.

Some of my other interlocutors spoke of nervousness, fatigue, and nightmares. Sara Ahmed suggests that race structures the body's mode of operation, and in these examples, we catch bodies in the act of racialization—when a boy avoids eye contact or takes off his hoodie as he boards the bus or when a young man shaves his beard before traveling or avoids having heritage food in public. Race structures those actions not prior to or after the hostile white gaze but during the exchange.[12] It is in these moments that whiteness becomes manifest as a modality of power and control. Racialization thus weighs down boys like Bilal and Faisal—a burden that they are forced to carry from a very young age. Black Muslim boys, as

---

12. Ahmed, "A Phenomenology of Whiteness," 153.

Faisal's comment suggests, may be aware of this burden through both distinct and overlapping routes and structures of feeling.

This weighed-down, racialized body—the postures it assumes, the clothes it puts on or takes off when entering public spaces, the accent it speaks in, the emotions it hides—thus becomes the matter through which the effect of whiteness appears in the world. But we also see how Black and Brown Muslims relate to whiteness in modes that are both like and unlike those of other boys of color. When Faisal (a Brown Muslim) suggests there is a "Muslim version" of the talk about police brutality, he illustrates how his experience overlaps with that of Black boys. But Bilal's comments about ICE raids—or when other Brown Muslim boys describe being labeled "terrorists" or being mocked for their accents, their food, or their parents' clothes—show that they also experience whiteness differently than their Black coreligionists. We are thus reminded of Deleuze and Guattari (from chapter 1) who point to variation within experiences of racialization. None of what I have written here is to argue against the reality that the American carceral logics are constructed to contain Black life—that is, in fact, its originary purpose, as Simone Browne shows in *Dark Matters*.[13] Instead, what I hope to have demonstrated is how that regime encloses numerous others constituted as nonwhite, even as it continues to be most heavily restrictive toward those coded as Black. Ultimately these surveillance practices leave an indelible mark on the surveilled.

Ironically, the afterschool program where I met these Muslim boys aims to enable them to integrate better into the society that encloses them. The program advertises that it will guide participants on "valuable skills such as personal finance and negotiation." It mobilizes the category of "underserved youth" to direct youth of color toward the ends of capitalism. Soo Ah Kwon thus suggests that we view such nonprofits as technologies of neoliberal governance that limit the development of oppositional political activism

13. Browne, *Dark Matters*.

in youth.[14] And yet, even though the teens in my focus groups had come together under a program with such evidently neoliberal goals, their comments above indicate that these programs may also become sites where they develop a consciousness of their marginality. In the years since 2017, some of my focus group members have gone on to become social activists and leaders in their own right. Nonprofits or community organizations indeed facilitate the production of self-governing subjects within a neoliberal state. But as entities that gather together members of "underserved" Black and Brown populations, they can also exist as spaces for consciousness-raising among them.

Muslim Boyhood in India

While the specific racial and capitalist logics that I have discussed thus far are those of the contemporary United States, Muslim boyhood is similarly constructed in other global contexts by powerful political and social entities that define themselves against and through it. As a heuristic device, Muslim boyhood enables us to discern linkages across political contexts even as its iterations take shape in locally specific ways and are networked with different genealogies. In the spirit of the present Forerunners series and its orientation toward speculation, I close with a meditation on the politics that Muslim boyhood reveals in contemporary India, where the ruling political party espouses the supremacist ideology of Hindutva.

Crafting an Uncontaminated Hindu Rashtra *(Nation)*

A video circulated in March 2021, first in India and eventually worldwide. It showed a teenage boy being slapped, kicked, and shoved to the ground by an adult man. The boy, it was later revealed,

14. Soo Ah Kwon, *Uncivil Youth* (Durham, N.C.: Duke University Press, 2013).

was a thirteen-year-old Muslim named Asif, who had entered a Hindu temple in Ghaziabad, India, looking for a drink of water. When caretaker Shringi Yadav asked the boy to identify himself and heard a Muslim name in response, he began to beat him. Another temple caretaker, Shivanand Saraswati, recorded the incident and posted it on social media with the caption: "*Mulle ko napunsak bana diya.*" *Mulle* is used as a disparaging term for Muslims (even though *mullah* technically refers to Muslims who are learned in Quran and theology). The term here appears within the caption's broader insult: "Muslim has been made impotent."[15] As Asif is beaten, he cries over and over: "I had come to drink water, uncle."

The temple caretaker's vicious beating of Asif—a thirsty boy in search of water—was obviously disproportionate to the offense of entering the temple without permission. In that, it resembles the incident at Dulles airport with which I opened this book: why beat or detain a boy who obviously poses no threat to two adult guards (or, in the Dulles incident, to an airport staffed by dozens of armed security)? Why record the beating and post it on social media? What work is the video supposed to do?

The online response demonstrated an effort to reduce the disparity between Asif's actions and the caretakers' (over)reactions by building up the boy's supposed offense. Some suggested the Ghaziabad temple caretakers beat Asif not because he had entered the temple, but because of actions he had allegedly taken within its walls. They claimed he was caught spitting; others alleged he had urinated in the temple space. Spit, blood, mucus, urine, and feces are of course viewed as polluting and pollutants, to be excreted from the body, flushed away. Spitting/urinating, in this narrative, sullied the purity of the temple and thus would justify the harsh discipline directed at the boy. But focusing on alleged behaviors

15. Bobins Abraham, "Muslim Boy Assaulted for Drinking Water from a Temple In UP," *India Times*, March 13, 2021, https://www.indiatimes.com /news/india/muslim-boy-assaulted-for-drinking-water-from-a-temple-in -up-accused-arrested-after-viral-video-536221.html.

elides the context in which the beating began—in the moment when Asif shared his legibly Muslim name. Asif had apparently ignored multiple signs outside the temple that prohibited Muslims from entering—or, perhaps more likely, as one news anchor pointed out, Asif was illiterate and thus could not read the warning signs.[16] However he came to be within its walls, the boy's entire being was unwelcome in the temple; spitting or urinating would be beside the point, since he himself was a pollutant. We can see in this incident how the Muslim boy presents a risk to the purity of the Hindu temple much in the same way as the Muslim boy, in its proto-terrorist formation, represents a risk to the nation's security in the American context. Both iterations of Muslim boyhood gain force through the construction and surveillance of domains of purity/impurity, innocence/threat.

The temple's exclusionary logic is more readily understood if we situate it within the current political landscape of India, where the ruling party now espouses and promulgates an ethnoreligious ideology in which Muslims are viewed *en masse* as contaminating, as matter out of place, as bodies to be expelled from India. Variously called *Hindutva* (literally, the essence of the Hindu) or Hindu nationalism, this political philosophy calls for the Indian state to be reorganized according to exclusively "Hindu" precepts.[17] As Chetan Bhatt and Parita Mukta explain, this worldview ascribes nationhood to Aryan and non-Aryan people on the subcontinent—inclusive of not only Hindus of different castes but also Jains, Buddhists, and Sikhs who have religions with roots in India—while excluding Christians and Muslims. The logic is premised on an assumption that Hindus share a common descent and are connected by blood

16. MOJO Story, "India's Islamophobia," *YouTube*, March 15, 2021, https://www.youtube.com/watch?v=om_Sc5mr4uc.

17. Chetan Bhatt and Parita Mukta, "Hindutva in the West: Mapping the Antinomies of Diaspora Nationalism," *Ethnic and Racial Studies* 23, no. 3 (2000): 407–41.

to the ancient Vedic-Aryan forefathers.[18] While Christians and Muslims may claim India as their country of birth (*pitrabhumi*), they cannot affiliate with it as the country of their religious traditions (*punyabhumi*), and hence their loyalty is always suspect.[19] In a Hindu *rashtra* (nation) as thus conceived, the Muslim remains a forever foreigner, in a formulation not dissimilar to the articulation of Muslims in America. In fact, as Shruti Devgan has shown, even within its broader Aryan and non-Aryan parameters, those included in the Hindu *rashtra* do not partake equally in its claimed purity; Sikhs are simultaneously included and excluded, incorporated in the Indian Constitution as "Hindu," but denied "authenticity" as Hindu by being cast as its "variant," especially as "separatist Khalistanis," when it suits the Indian state.[20] In this sense, racialization in India unfolds through similar patterns that we saw in the American case: where nonconforming traits (or religious groups in this instance) are integrated in "increasingly eccentric and backward waves" in relation to a center.[21] The Hindutva ideology is not new; it emerged in the 1920s as an upper-caste ideology. But it is now widespread due to the political and cultural efforts of organizations such as the Hindu Mahasabha and Rashtriya Swayamsevak Sangh (RSS). India's present ruling party, Bharatiya Janata, traces its roots to Jan Sangh, the political arm of the right-wing RSS, which was launched in the early 1950s.

In the Hindutva worldview, religious minorities like Muslims must either be exterminated or assimilated, with the latter demon-

18. Bhatt and Mukta, 413.

19. As explicated by nationalist Vinayak Savarkar in *Hindutva: Who Is a Hindu?;* see also Christophe Jaffrelot, "The Idea of Hindu Race in the Writings of Hindu Nationalist Ideologues in the 1920s and 1930s: A Concept between Two Cultures," in *The Concept of Race in South Asia,* ed. Peter Robb (Delhi: Oxford University Press, 1995), 327–54.

20. Shruti Devgan, "'Give In, Cut Your Hair . . . Or It Makes You a Very Strong Person,'" in *Sociology of South Asia,* ed. Smitha Radhakrishnan and Gowri Vijayakumar (Cham, Switz.: Palgrave Macmillan, 2022), 205–32.

21. Deleuze and Guattari, *A Thousand Plateaus,* 178.

strated by unconditional obeisance. Both routes—extermination/ expulsion and absorption/assimilation—retain and enforce the center (purity of the Hindu *rashtra*). If we consider the Hindu temple at Ghaziabad as a material site that concretizes the ideology of Hindutva—and spaces of worship are often seen as material manifestations of religious ideologies—then Asif breached the purity that the temple represented and sought to foster (through signage to exclude Muslims, for example). The temple also becomes a site where Muslim presence is imagined as threatening Hindu women's sexual purity—a theme that resonates with the American- or European-imagined Muslim threat to white women discussed earlier. When the head priest of the Ghaziabad temple rationalized Asif's beating, he noted that in the past Muslims had sexually harassed female devotees.[22] At work here is not only the sexualization of a supposed "threat" represented by Muslim boys—discussed at length above— but also a further discourse popularly known in India as "love jihad." In the imaginary of love jihad, Muslim youth seduce Hindu women and convert them to Islam in an effort to "Islamize" India.

Against this background, the caretaker's kicks and shoves were meant not only for Asif as a particular Muslim youth but also for the witnessing public, both online and offline. Shringi intentionally kicks Asif's genital area; we see the boy trying to protect it with his left hand. In that moment we see an explicit act of violence and an implicit act of erasure. Shringi's violence was both purposeful and didactic. As the video begins, we hear Shringi tell his colleague to make sure their faces can be seen. When his colleague Shivanand posts the video on social media with text celebrating the beating as making the boy "impotent," that too is instructive: the two men had punished the boy for his infraction and claimed—in a reversal of the love jihad imaginary—to have destroyed his progeny (made

22. OpIndia Staff, "This Temple Has Been Robbed Four Times," *OpIndia*, March 16, 2021, https://www.opindia.com/2021/03/ghaziabad -dasna-temple-asif-slapped-hindu-temple-mahant-killed-muslims-entry -water/.

him impotent) reducing the chance of further incursions of Hindu space in the future. While an adult Muslim man might already have children, a thirteen-year-old boy likely does not: to render him impotent would thus eradicate an entire line of future Muslims. In this orientation to the future (the destruction of future Muslims), the Indian reaction against Muslim boys resembles its American iteration, where enclosure and surveillance of Muslim boys is imagined as eliminating future terror.

A fixation on Muslim fertility (and relatedly, futurity) is an enduring feature of Hindutva discourse. Shringi had reportedly advocated for controlling the "rising population" of minority communities.[23] When a reporter suggested to the temple's head priest that Asif was likely unable to read the sign barring Muslims from the temple, the priest's response jumped right to birth rates: "What is the point of raising so many children if they can't even provide basic literacy? Is it to commit theft, robbery, and loot?"[24] A similar criticism of Muslim families (mothers in particular) is evident in another video that went viral on August 25, 2023.[25] In this incident, which took place at Neha Public School in Uttar Pradesh, we see a seven-year-old Muslim boy being hit and slapped by his peers, while a teacher sitting in the background encourages the students to hit him harder. When one student slaps the seven-year-old on the face, the teacher tells the next one to hit him on the back too. The Muslim child can

23. Abhijay Jha, "Boy Beaten Up Badly for Entering Temple for Water," *Sunday Times of India*, March 14, 2021.

24. As quoted in OpIndia Staff, "This Temple Has Been Robbed Four Times."

25. Muslim Daily (@Muslimdaily_), "India may have made it to the moon but millions of Muslims still don't have basic rights as Muslims are lynched in public sight. In this school the teacher asks Hindu children to slap a Muslim child, even berating them if they don't slap hard enough," Twitter, August 25, 2023, 12:49 p.m., https://twitter.com/muslimdaily_ /status/1695116083521339475; Faisal Meer, "Outrage in India over Video of Teacher Telling Kids to Slap Muslim Student," *AlJazeera News*, August 25, 2023, https://www.aljazeera.com/news/2023/8/25/outrage-in-india-over -video-of-teacher-telling-kids-to-slap-muslim-student.

now be seen wailing. The teacher Tripta Tyagi says: "I have declared that all the Mohammedan children whose mothers have left or are not present, their lives have been ruined." And the person making the video (allegedly another teacher) agrees. During an investigation later on, the teacher maintained that she did not single out the child for being a Muslim but media commentators disagreed. As journalist Barkha Dutt retorted: "Let me tell you why mentioning the religion of the child is critical. Because in the same video the schoolteacher actually makes a reference to Muslims. She uses the word 'Mohammadan,' an old-style word, to reference the Muslim community."[26]

Within the Hindutva imaginary, the rising population of Muslims signifies a threat to the integrity of the body politic. Muslim biological and cultural reproduction therefore often becomes a point of denigration. In this viewpoint, a healthy and harmonious body/polity is not a given, but must be actively produced, cared for, and attended to. Citizens—from temple guards to teachers—and state institutions are accordingly obligated to protect the body from corrupt elements both within and outside its borders. And some, including Hindu Mahasabha political party member Pooja Shakun Pandey, have argued that antidemocratic measures and even genocide of Muslims could be justified by this supposed obligation.[27]

The mother of the seven-year-old boy beaten at school said: "Yesterday, my son came home crying . . . He was traumatized. This is not how you treat kids."[28] And, when a news anchor on MOJO asked a heavily bandaged Asif if he would ever go to the temple again, the boy said no: *"Nahi. Ab hamare dil main dehshat behthi [hai]. Ab dobara ghar say hum bahir nahi gaen gayi.* (No, now there

26. Barkha Dutt, "UP Viral Video," *YouTube*, August 26, 2023, https://www.youtube.com/watch?v=3Vefa_z6rw8.

27. As cited in Rhea Mogul, "India's Hindu Extremists," *CNN News*, January 14, 2022, https://www.cnn.com/2022/01/14/asia/india-hindu-extremist-groups-intl-hnk-dst/index.html.

28. Meer, "Outrage in India over Video."

is fear in my heart. Now I will not leave home again)."[29] In these statements, we see a similar shrinking and reduction of Muslim life that we previously saw in the case of Muslim boys in America.

I have closed with this brief reflection on Muslim boyhood in India not to suggest an exhaustive comparative study of this altogether different context, but to gesture toward some overlaps and commonalities. We observe how racial supremacy, carceral logics, and sexual/reproductive anxiety shape iterations of Muslim boyhood while also noticing its locally specific genealogies. Whether authorities detain a five-year-old at an airport in Washington, D.C., or ordinary citizens beat up a thirteen-year-old at a temple in Ghaziabad, these actions are aimed less at punishing current transgressions and more toward eliminating imagined future ones. These scattered illustrations show how purity and innocence may be centered differently on concerns around reproduction, terrorism, immigrants stealing jobs, or racial supremacy, across global contexts, and yet Muslim boyhood may serve as a useful heuristic device to investigate their workings. This exercise can also helpfully illustrate the synergies between different nationalist projects. Examining activism of members of the "Hindus for Trump" group alongside alt-right groups in the United States, Sitara Thobani argues that both projects rely on public construction of alterity epitomized by the Muslim other.[30] Khaled Beydoun has likewise traced transnational connections by examining how the American War on Terror became a vehicle for exporting the fear of Islam to places such as India and China.[31] A close examination of Muslim boyhood in different global contexts

29. MOJO Story, "India's Islamophobia."

30. Sitara Thobani, "Alt-Right with the Hindu-right: Long-Distance Nationalism and the Perfection of Hindutva," *Ethnic and Racial Studies* 42, no. 5 (2019): 747.

31. Khaled Beydoun, "Exporting Islamophobia in the Global 'War of Terror,'" *New York University Law Review* 95, no. 81 (2020): 81–100.

can show how the fears that Beydoun talks about merge and interact with longstanding local discourses about the Muslim other.

I have not tried to argue that Muslim boys should be granted access to the domain of innocence. Innocence is a disciplinary framework, and its production relies on a blameworthy other. I have been more interested in the politics of innocence and purity: if innocence (as a "space of purity," per Ticktin) as an ideology will not be abandoned, and we continue to recognize suffering as valid only when it is experienced by those we categorize as innocent, then exclusion from the protective domain of innocence produces conditions that leave ordinary Muslim boys broadly vulnerable to violence. In elaborating the confluence of racial, capitalist, and carceral logics that sustain the political formation(s) of Muslim boyhood as a threat, my hope is not to simply document it but to issue a call for urgent action. Ultimately, what is at stake is Muslim life. Muslim boys in the United States (and India) today are denied the opportunity to experiment and fail, to experience joy and gain knowledge, to assert agency while also seeking care. It is impossible for Muslim boys to experience childhood and youth as the messy time that it often is—and thus Muslim boyhood itself becomes a truncated experience, a harbinger of premature death. As the high school boys I spoke with were well aware, Muslim life in America is a diminished life, defined by surveillance and by social and political exclusion.

Acknowledgments

Alhamdu li-llahi rabbil alamin.

This book emerges from a decade-long reflection on Muslim youth, particularly boys, in America. I am grateful to my interlocutors—Muslim boys from Queens, New York—who shared their experiences with me, as well as boys and men whom I engaged with for other research projects but whose experiences have shaped my interpretation and sharpened my analysis for this project as well.

I thank my teachers Monisha Bajaj, Nancy Lesko, and Lila Abu-Lughod for their helpful guidance. I am grateful to Saher Selod, Jay Sosa, Shruti Devgan, Julia Boss, Mariam Durrani, Karishma Desai, and Mary Ann Chacko for reading drafts and sharing invaluable feedback. Salimah Shamsuddin, the Director of Resettlement and Integration Programs at Lutheran Social Services, shared her insights about the Afghan refugee resettlement process; Matti Gellman shared important updates on Rezwan Kohistani's case; Ryan Zohar at Georgetown University Library was extremely helpful in securing court rulings and other legal documents; and Erum Jaffer facilitated introductions to South Asian youth in New York. I have benefited from many conversations with colleagues and friends: thank you, Celene Ibrahim, Alyssa Niccolini, Stephanie McCall, and Bessie Dernikos. I am grateful to my colleagues at Georgetown University, and in particular the staff at the Alwaleed

Bin Talal Center for Muslim-Christian Understanding, for their support. Many thanks to Leah Pennywark and Anne Carter, my wonderful editors at the University of Minnesota Press, and the production team of the Forerunners: Ideas First series.

Finally, my deep gratitude to my family for their support.

(Continued from page iii)

Forerunners: Ideas First

Claudia Milian
LatinX

Aaron Jaffe
Spoiler Alert: A Critical Guide

Don Ihde
Medical Technics

Jonathan Beecher Field
Town Hall Meetings and the Death of Deliberation

Jennifer Gabrys
How to Do Things with Sensors

Naa Oyo A. Kwate
Burgers in Blackface: Anti-Black Restaurants Then and Now

Arne De Boever
Against Aesthetic Exceptionalism

Steve Mentz
Break Up the Anthropocene

John Protevi
Edges of the State

Matthew J. Wolf-Meyer
Theory for the World to Come: Speculative Fiction and Apocalyptic Anthropology

Nicholas Tampio
Learning versus the Common Core

Kathryn Yusoff
A Billion Black Anthropocenes or None

Kenneth J. Saltman
The Swindle of Innovative Educational Finance

Ginger Nolan
The Neocolonialism of the Global Village

Joanna Zylinska
The End of Man: A Feminist Counterapocalypse

Robert Rosenberger
Callous Objects: Designs against the Homeless

William E. Connolly
Aspirational Fascism: The Struggle for Multifaceted Democracy under Trumpism

Shenila Khoja-Moolji is the Hamad bin Khalifa al-Thani Associate Professor of Muslim Societies at Georgetown University. Her books include *Forging the Ideal Educated Girl: The Production of Desirable Subjects in Muslim South Asia*; *Sovereign Attachments: Masculinity, Muslimness, and Affective Politics in Pakistan*; and *Rebuilding Community: Displaced Women and the Making of a Shia Ismaili Muslim Sociality*.